D1584990

Writers of Wales

EDITORS

MEIC STEPHENS   R. BRINLEY JONES

DAVID JONES

1895–1974

René Hague

DAVID

JONES

University of Wales Press
on behalf of the Welsh Arts Council

1975

41302

I

Introductory

I found, when I set out to write about David
Jones, that I needed a double form of introduction: an introduction for the reader, which
might serve to tell him what person it was that I
wished him to greet, and an introduction for the
writer, too, which would lead him into the
subject—a springboard, in fact, for both of us, to
launch us smoothly into the deep end. And as I
cast about for an appropriate exordium, I came
upon a passage in the autobiography of a common
friend which fulfils the double purpose far better
than anything I could devise myself. In his ONE
THING AT A TIME, Harman Grisewood has been
speaking of the long discussions that used to go on
in a circle of friends, all much of the same age—
David rather senior to most of us—and of the
special authority which David's contribution
gained from his position as a 'working artist': and
he continues:

'Art, religion, history were our themes. If this or that
appreciation or proposition is true aesthetically, does it weaken
or support, we would ask, this other proposition in terms of the
Christian religion? Every experience, emotional or intellectual,
had to be discussed from the standpoints of art, religion,
history, until there was only one standpoint or, which was the
usual conclusion, David Jones had to catch the last train home
from Blackfriars to Brockley . . . David Jones had the skill and
learning to be a literary artist in the conventional style. He
knew what he was doing in his experiment. He chose the mode

1

of it for an artist's reasons, but he was more conscious of them than most artists are, and he could discuss them objectively . . . The whole of him had to consent in the artist's decisions—the Catholic, the man of taste, the man of reason, the historian, the patriot, the soldier . . . His maxim, " The artist must be dead to himself while engaged upon the work", involves in his case a Herculean act of self-restraint because he is alive to so much. Had he never put brush or pen to paper he would have led the life of an artist in himself.'

The date is 1930–31, and the place at which one particular group of conversations referred to took place was, appropriately, Welsh—Caldey Island, off Tenby, where David had been joined by two friends; and even more appropriately (almost inevitably, in view of the date) the third participant was Tom Burns: for Tom added to the blaze of intelligence the power that most of us lacked, to convert wishes and plans into action. He was a publisher, and so he was our public, or semi-public spokesman. In a rather openly clandestine way he was responsible for the periodical ORDER (*'We are here to discuss among ourselves order—that is, arrangement in some English Catholic affairs'*), whose four issues are now coveted by those who were not wise enough to save their own copies. (David's association with ORDER was immediately apparent from the engraving on the cover of the unicorn in the 'garden enclosed': themes that constantly recur in his work.) ORDER, in a general way, expressed the demand of the intelligent Christian to introduce into his religion and its practice the same intellectual responsibility that he sought to exercise in what were marked off as 'secular' affairs; and, in a more particular way, it tried to clear away the mass of

2

pietistic rubbish, devotional, architectural, institutional, which cluttered up Church and churches. At the same time Tom, in his normal work, published, among many other valuable writers new to English readers, three who are of particular importance in connection with David Jones and those with whom he associated at this time: Jacques Maritain,[1] Maurice de la Taille, and Christopher Dawson; and these three, it will be noted, coincide with the three subjects of discussion mentioned in the quotation above—art, religion, and history. How wide and deep David's reading has been is apparent (quite apart from the endless references that may be unearthed in his work) from the random list that poured from his pen when, in the preface to the ANATHEMATA, he paid tribute to those who *'have aided us in our artefacts'*; but the three writers mentioned have been central. It is interesting, incidentally, that David uses that phrase, *'aided us in our artefacts'*; for the plural shows, or at least hints, that he is thinking of the artificer as a unit in a basically poetic mankind—that *poiesis* is the normal mark of man as such—and the help he acknowledges reminds us that those writers provided not only a framework or background to which his own experiences and sensibilities could be related, but also to some degree the very material of his poetry.

This period of the late twenties and early thirties was one of great activity for David as painter and

---

[1] Though David, it is true, first read Maritain's ART ET SCOLASTIQUE in the shorter, and more eccentric, version translated by Fr. John O'Connor, and printed and published by Hilary Pepler, under the title THE PHILOSOPHY OF ART.

3

engraver. This was the vigorous, enquiring, pertinacious, artificer—a man of great jest, of wry gaiety, and yet of deep seriousness, constantly troubled by the excess of man's reach over his grasp, some reflection of whose personality I am trying to show the reader; and I have chosen this particular date because it was one of the peaks of his long career, and was the first time when he had completely emerged from any form of tutelage or apprenticeship and was master in his own domain. There is the further reason that in those years—starting, in fact, somewhat earlier—I was myself in close contact with David, and, after my marriage in 1930, he for some time shared a home with my wife Joan and me: and so we had the great privilege of his comradeship. For it has always been one of David's great virtues that, for all his inevitable concentration on his own work and its problems, he could share in, and offer a share of, an ever-reliable, sympathetic and encouraging friendship. There are a few persons, and he is one, who have this gift of making their friend feel that he is more gifted than he is, more interesting, more learned, cleverer: and the effect of their companionship is, in fact, to enable the friend to develop those qualities to a degree he never possessed before. I associate David with domestic life in a very small house, washing-up, squaring away the room, fetching wood for the fire, blocking patient Joan's way into the kitchen by standing at his work in the very narrow little passageway: for David, so far as I know, never worked out of doors (and he produced a great many watercolours at Pigotts)—that would have brought bitter oaths and complaints about wind, sun, insects *('enough blank trouble getting the blank thing right without struggling with the blank elements').*

Eric Gill, with his wife Mary and his two unmarried daughters, Petra and Joan, and his young son Gordian, had moved from Capel-y-ffin (of which more later) to Pigotts in 1928; and it may be as well to have some idea of what sort of place it was. It lay some 5 miles from High Wycombe in Buckinghamshire, on the road first to Speen and then Princes Risborough: an old brick Bucks farmhouse, long neglected, which Eric had repaired and made into a sound and workmanlike collection of dwelling houses and workshops (he had a genius in such work for getting everything exactly right, logical, aptly fitted to time and place). The buildings formed a quadrangle: one side was what we called the big house, in which Eric and Mary lived; a second, divided from it by the chapel (what a luxury to look back on in these days of vernacular prayer-meetings) formed Eric's stone and engraving workshops; a third was mostly a one-storied building in which we had started printing (afterwards it was occupied by the late Bernard Wall—God rest him—and his wife Barbara; few friends were so close to David, both emotionally and intellectually, as Bernard); not long after the arrival at Pigotts, Petra married Denis Tegetmeier, and they lived, and Denis had his workshop, in the fourth side. Projecting from that was a curious little cottage in which Joan and I lived after we were married, and so at times did David. Before that, during most of 1930, if my memory is correct, David and I shared a room over Eric's engraving room: it was entered by a step-ladder and a trap-door, and we called it the billet; this little bachelor enclave had, indeed, a most billet-like quality. It was from the window of this room that David drew 'Pigotts in storm', which is reproduced in the little book in the 'Penguin Modern Painters' series. It looks across the yard, as we called the quadrangle, at the Tegetmeiers', and the left-hand dormer window as you look at that building is the window of David's billet when he was with us in the cottage. There is an interesting relic of Pigotts in David's most recently published poems, THE SLEEPING LORD: in 'The Book of Balaam's Ass' (which originated well before THE ANATHEMATA)—

'of Hycga their tall father, who burned twelve Welshmen with fire in Piggots garth and had his oats in Speen. These three chair-makers' mates moved lightfoot from Fricourt to Highwood saying: There's nothing like chalk to dance on.'

In a note David says that Jutes in the vicinity of High Wycombe sounds improbable, but I have a vague memory of a conversation on which the reference is based. The spelling 'Piggots' is interesting as an indication of the date of composition, for we changed it later, for con-venience in writing, and to match the local pronunciation, to Pigotts; I have seen it printed on a map as they pronounced it, Pycotts. 'Garth' is interesting, too, for the word must have come to David, as applied to that sort of quadrangle, from the monastery at Capel-y-ffin. There we inherited the name 'garth' from the founder of the monastery, Fr. Ignatius, for whom the word must have had a more authentically 'monastic ring: while for David the association with the O.E. *geard* (i.e. yard) was precisely what was needed.

And Wycombe, of course, has for many years
been a great centre for chair-making. In our day
the 'bodger' could still be seen at work in the
beech woods, turning chair legs on a simple
lathe powered by a bent sapling. And the
Chilterns, moreover, are chalk country.

London and Pigotts are rather apt to run together
in memory after more than forty years, and
looking back at the mid-twenties and early
thirties they assume a sort of period quality: the
three friends referred to earlier, gathered in what
now seems almost the equivalent of a Victorian
or Edwardian 'reading party'; the ash sticks we
carried, in London, in our gloved hands; the
wide-brimmed hats; the shabby flannels (though
here I speak only of myself: for David, though
never smart and with only a limited wardrobe,
always wore very *good* clothes, very sound—his
shoes, in particular, were of fine leather, excel-
lently sewn and aptly built, as one would expect
in a man with such respect for the artificer); the
meals in Soho that were cheap even by our
poverty-stricken standards; the trams diving
underground by the Central School and emerging
on the Embankment; walking with David to
Blackfriars Station; the mirrored Adam and Eve
—these, in retrospect, produce an atmosphere of
eighty or ninety years ago rather than forty or
fifty. These were the days before ill-health had
done so much to hamper David; and, whatever
interior self-questionings may have been going
on, there was—as there continued to be in each
new flare-up of energy—a great certainty and
assurance in his work. He would, it is true,
probably disclaim those qualities, being too

modest to recognise them in the result, and too conscious of the amount of pushing, pulling, fitting, re-adjusting, jettisoning, salvaging, the combination of ferocity and delicacy, that his drawing, painting or writing has called for. In engraving the process can be observed in the unfinished 'He frees the waters' reproduced (not too badly but much reduced) in the ANATHEMATA, particularly if this is compared with the elaborate, and finished, engraving 'Everyman'. Another most instructive example is the comparatively recent watercolour drawing—one of the really substantial pieces, like 'Aphrodite in Aulis' and 'Vexilla Regis', which astound you by their richness and weight—'The Kensington Mass', a companion to the poem of the same title, a draft of which was printed in the 1974 David Jones issue of AGENDA. This started as a loose, fluid, water-colour on comparatively light paper; came close to being rejected; was mounted on heavier paper, enlarged both laterally and longitudinally; was worked over in body-colour and pencil; and ended up with the same amalgam of nicety and solidity as is found in the great pieces with which I associated it. The process could not be observed in his poetry without examination of the mass of manuscript that has accumulated in his various billets, but he has described it himself on more than one occasion. Writing (in the Preface) of THE ANATHEMATA he says that

'It had its beginnings in experiments made from time to time between 1938 and 1945. In a sense what was then written is another book. It has been rewritten, large portions excluded, others added, the whole rearranged and considerably changed more than once. I find, for instance, that what is now sheet 166

8

of my written MS has at different times been sheet 75 and sheet 7. What is now printed represents parts, dislocated attempts, reshuffled and again rewritten intermittently . . .'

And in a letter David writes (in July 1973):

'. . . *when, in 1928 at Portslade in Sussex I began to find out for myself in what way the making of a writing presented other problems of "form" and "content" as compared with those same problems that I had every reason to know constitute the main, or rather the whole, problem in the visual arts. I began what ultimately came to be I.P. with no other idea than to find out in what fashion these problems of "form" and "content" cropped up in the totally different media of written words. It's hard to make chaps believe this, because they can't seem to see that this business of making a thing inevitably involves this marriage of "form" and "content" no matter whether the thing made is a painting or some visual artwork. So also it must crop up in making a writing. They tend to say, Well, you may have been, previous to 1928, entirely concerned with the visual arts, but you must have read a fair amount of stuff. That may be true enough (but even if true it misses the point), but a bloke may spend hours, months, years looking at visual works of all sorts, from the marvel of Irish metal work of the 7th century or an astounding illuminated Irish ms, or, to get poles apart, some kouros or parthenos of Hellenic antiquity, but let him try to make an object of twisted gold or script on vellum & he'll find he's up against this matter of "form" and "content". And the only possible way is to have a crack at making some confounded thing with your own hands. For me, in the case of my first attempts at making a writing, it was much the same, only the other way round. I began, as far as I can remember, with making a drawing and writing some stuff to go with it. But soon gave up the idea and got immersed in the difficulties inherent in the writing.'*

9

The interest of this letter has led me somewhat further than I intended, into the writing of IN PARENTHESIS; and it may be as well to step back a few years in time and speak of Eric Gill, Ditchling, and Capel-y-ffin in 1924.

II

Capel-y-ffin

I have so far refrained from giving any biographical details of David, because I wanted the man himself to appear, actually engaged in his work. Moreover, it has been better and more conveniently done elsewhere: David's own short autobiographical talk (reprinted in EPOCH AND ARTIST) says all that needs to be said, particularly if it is supplemented (and this applies most to Welsh readers) by a very moving letter in the periodical PLANET (No. 21, January 1974). Valuable and conveniently arranged is the 'Word and Image' catalogue compiled by Douglas Cleverdon (published by the National Book League), which lists a large number of important works chronologically, and reproduces many, and at the same time gives a running biographical and explanatory commentary, much of it in David's own words taken from conversation and letters. But as I now want to get David into the Black Mountains of the Radnor-Brecon-Monmouth borders in 1924, let me briefly recapitulate what may be read more fully elsewhere.

David Jones (not David Michael, as some would have it)[1] was born at Brockley in Kent (as it then was) on 1st November 1895. The Welshness of his father and the Englishness of his mother he has

---

[1] He took the additional name of Michael when he was received into the Catholic Church in November 1921, the feast of St. Michael being close at hand.

described himself. His formal education amounted to little, but from a very early age, when he was no more than six years old, there was no time when, in his own words *'drawing of some sort was not an accustomed activity and one which I supposed I should pursue later in life'.*[1] When he was only 14 he went to the Camberwell Art School, and was a student there in 1914 at the outbreak of war. There was some delay in forming a London Welsh battalion of the Royal Welch Fusiliers (his father wrote to Lloyd George about this, and received an answer counselling patience), but he was attested as '579 Jones on 2nd January 1915; embarked for France in December 1915; went up the line to the La Bassée sector; marched south in the summer of 1916 to take part in the Somme offensive; was wounded in the attack on Mametz Wood of 10th July (or more exactly in the early hours of 11th July); returned to England; back to France; suffered from trench fever; and his last posting was to Limerick, whence he was demobilised soon after the armistice in 1918.

With a government grant, David then went to the Westminster School of Art, in 1919, and it was from there that he went to join Eric Gill, first at Ditchling in Sussex and, in 1924, at Capel-y-ffin. His parents' home in Brockley was more or less his permanent base (though with long absences)

---

[1] One small memory may be of interest: David's earliest full recollection of the outside world as a small child (little more than four years old) is the relief of Mafeking on 17th February 1900, his father being roused in the middle of the night to make the necessary corrections in the paper on which he was then working as a printers' overseer.

until his mother's death in 1937. The nearest approach to a home—and by 'home' is meant not a domestic establishment but a place where a man can collect and keep and use and hunt through his gear—since Brockley, was a fine large room he had in Northwick Lodge, Harrow on the Hill, to which he went in 1946. Before this, in the early days of the second war, he had a sort of dug-out in Sheffield Terrace, Notting Hill Gate. When Northwick Lodge was condemned to demolition, David moved into a small hotel in Harrow, and it was there that in 1970 he fell and broke his hip; and since then he has lived in a convent nursing home on the hill of Harrow. He spent, however, a lot of time in other parts of England and Wales— at Ditchling and Portslade in Sussex, at Capel-y-ffin and Caldey Island in Wales, at Sidmouth, at Pigotts, and at Helen Sutherland's (mostly at Rock in Northumberland, but later at Cockley Moor, near Troutbeck). He was also for a time in France, in the Basses Pyrénées, in Egypt and in what was then called Palestine. All these places (except Sidmouth and the Near East, I think, and with little surviving from Ditchling) are reflected in his watercolours: and many references to them, images or ideas suggested by them, are to be found in his writings. Jerusalem, in particular (as an example) provided the material for a key passage in THE ANATHEMATA—the water-carrier, and the cool upper room—and both writer and reader delight in a special recognition of such names, from the Honddu valley, as Powell Chapel Farm, Lewis the Vision, and Watkins Talsarn, in their juxtaposition with Luke's argument of the shepherd who searches for the one lost sheep out of the hundred: David's wonderful poetic monism, again, bringing all things into one.

And to these journeyings and visits must, of course, be added his war service in France and Ireland.

Capel-y-ffin lies at the head of the Honddu valley, which runs northward, narrowing, from Llanvihangel Crucorney, near Abergavenny, for some ten miles; until it is blocked by the rounded mass of the Tump, and forks. The left-hand fork becoming even more narrow and rising up to the escarpment of Rhiw Wen, where, as the ground drops steeply before you, you can look out over a wide expanse towards Talgarth and the Beacons. The right-hand fork is more open and leads, over Hay Bluff, to the Hay—the La Haie Taillée of THE SLEEPING LORD.[1] (The hill, and in particular the rounded hill, I think, has always been one of David's fundamental images: and this hill-name has persisted, so that we find him using it again in the late fifties or sixties, to appear in his marvellous prayer, 'The Tutelar of the Place':

'Tellus of the myriad names answers to but one name: From this tump she answers Jac o' the Tump only if he call Great-Jill-of-the-tump-that-bare-me, not if he cry by some new fangle moder of far gentes over the flud . . .')

In the 1870's a Benedictine monastery had been built at Capel-y-ffin by Joseph Leycester Lyne (generally known by his name in religion, Father

---

[1] Christopher Dawson, David reminds me, was born in Hay Castle.

Ignatius)[1]: a stone quadrangular building, the wooded lower or mid-slope of the mountain rising behind it (above that the bare rock and heather), the dingle (as we called it, importing from George Borrow a word foreign to those parts) enclosing another side with trees and running water. (Borrow has always been a favourite with David—'the man in black', 'go to Rome for money', 'tip him Long Melford', are phrases you have only to hint at to get a responsive twinkle from his bright brown eye. And he includes a fine piece on Borrow—written as an introduction to the Everyman edition of Wild Wales—in EPOCH AND ARTIST.) Over the hill at the back of the monastery ran the 'waterworks valley' (it had been dammed for a reservoir), more correctly Tarren yr Esgob—the bishop being Archbishop Baldwin, who journeyed there in 1182, preaching the crusade, accompanied by Giraldus Cambrensis. The monastery stands at a height of 1,300 feet and Pen y Gadair Fawr, which overlooks the bishop's valley, rises to just over 3,000 feet—water, timber, rock, and the great bulge of the Tump: a truly Davidian country, with, in his words *'the strong hill-rhythms and the bright counter-rhythms of the* afonydd dyfroedd *which makes of so much of Wales a "plurabelle"*.' A reader's delight in poetry cannot but be enhanced by an understanding of the things and places from which images have originated and with which they are

---

[1] For information concerning this idiosyncratic visionary who was greatly loved and respected in the valley, see Donald Attwater's FATHER IGNATIUS OF LLANTHONY, (London, 1931); and for the old Llanthony, Giraldus Cambrensis, Everyman edition (Hoare's translation, ed. W. Llewelyn Williams) chap. 3.

associated. If you see that valley, those mountain shapes, the rocks that both threaten and shelter, the trees that stop short in a sharp line as the height increases, the undulating line of the mountain wall which confines the sheep to the upper ground, you obtain a much fuller understanding of David's great hill-invocation (THE ANATHEMATA, p. 56), of the endless recessions opened up by the little cluster of words that precedes it

> *the stone*
> *the fonted water*
> *the fronded wood*

and David's note, with a characteristic Vergilian raid, on those lines.

It was Donald Attwater who first suggested that Eric Gill might move from Ditchling to Fr. Ignatius's monastery, which then belonged to the Benedictines of Caldey Island (the community which is now at Prinknash). He has given an excellent account of the valley itself and of the life we lived there (he and his family occupying one side of the building until 1927) in his book about Eric, A CELL OF GOOD LIVING (London, 1969). He had a deep understanding of the country and its inhabitants, the small sheep-farmers who shared the mountain pastures; and he is one of the few writers who have understood that Eric's only eccentricity was his logic, and have refrained from embroidering the narrative with legendary tourists' tales. He gives the best written account of the man whom David came to love and admire so deeply, just as Walter Shewring (in a book I shall be referring to later) gives much the best account of the social and philosophic ideas that Eric untiringly put forward.

This was very much a border country. There was no Welsh spoken, though the intonation was characteristically Welsh; and many fragments of Welsh names, in a corrupt and anglicised way, became part of our normal vocabulary—Pen-y-Maes, Maes-y-ffin, Tir Onnen, Tŷ Siors, the Broadley, Miss Lewis's Pitch (across which ran the Monmouth-Brecon border), The Vision (what did that represent, or Tintail?), Nant-y-Gwyddel, 'please to catch hold' (at the tea-table), 'tashing' wood for the hedgers, and 'glatting', 'gambol' for a four-wheeled waggon, the Blaenau (we imported that word into Buckinghamshire, applying it to outlying farm buildings).

'It was in the Black Mountains that I made some drawings that appear, in retrospect, to have marked a new beginning. My subsequent work can, I think, be truthfully said to hinge on that period. All my exhibited work dates from after that period, none, or virtually none, from before it.'

If the influence of Capel-y-ffin was strong in David's visual work, even more (if only because you can get hold of a book when you may be lucky even to see a reproduction of a picture) can it be recognised in his poetry. 'The Hunt', 'The Sleeping Lord', 'The Tutelar of the Place'—and many passages in IN PARENTHESIS and THE ANATHEMATA, of course—contain a number of direct references: and although that great mass of poetry draws upon many other diverse sources, it would not, I think, be untrue to say that at

Capel-y-ffin David began *clearly* to see a general pattern, historical, geological, cultural, significant, in the conformation of his loved island. *Significant,* in the sense of making or providing, or suggesting a sign: and a neat and simple example of this— one of many, which I quote because of David's interesting note—occurs in THE SLEEPING LORD (p. 90).

> *Tawny-black sky-scurries*
> > *low over*
>
> *Ysgyryd hill*
> *and over the level-topped heights of*
> > *Mynnydd Pen-y-fal*

'*I wondered*', writes David, '*whether you recognised in Ysgyryd hill the Skirrid of your famous song,* '*Frank Large of the Skirrid Inn*'. *It was a bit of luck that Ysgyryd hill, as said in Welsh,* '*chimes*' *pretty well with sky-scurries in the line above —and that Mynnydd Pen-y-Fal, again as said in Welsh, has an assonance with* '. . . *hill / and over the level-topped heights.*'

The Skirrid is a few miles from Abergavenny, on the Hereford road, looking at the entrance to the Nant Honddu; and the Sugar Loaf (Mynnydd Pen-y-fal) looms over Abergavenny itself.

Capel, however, must be preceded by Ditchling, and Ditchling (though this can again wait for the moment) by the Great War. David, soon after he had become a Catholic, went to join Eric at Ditchling in November 1921. He did not join the guild of craftsmen which had been founded by Eric and Hilary Pepler—printers, engravers, stone and wood-carvers, carpenters—but he did delib-erately detach himself from the lines on which

18

he had been running, the normal progress through the art school to emptiness, with the associated view of the artist as essentially different from, and superior to, the workman: not, indeed, that in the pre-Ditchling days he necessarily shared that view of the arts, but he had been moving in circles in which no other view would have been generally entertained. Ditchling, was, I imagine, a period of escape, retirement, and development. There is always an impertinence in describing another man's views and feelings, however close one may have been to him: and looking back on what I have just said, I am very conscious of this; but I am comforted by the knowledge that, particularly in what concerns David's views on man-the-maker, any distortion of his view may be corrected by what he has said himself in EPOCH AND ARTIST.

At first David worked under George Maxwell, builder and joiner, and it is said (David himself may even have said it) that *'he was a total failure as a carpenter'*. This is hard to believe. You have only to look at a wooden object made by David, from the most utilitarian (and yet, how difficult are words and ideas: it is almost a contradiction in terms to speak of David's making a utilitarian object—but let the word stand for now)—from the most utilitarian (a door-latch, a spoon and fork) to the most extra-utile (to use his own term), a little wooden torso, a boxwood carving, a three or four-foot oak St. Dominic, to see in it a respect for, and knowledge of, the material, a logical assessment of the rational solution to the problem of making what is needed, combined with that extra, gratuitous, curious, *twist*—which distinguishes it from the functional—which is impossible to define—which is personal and characteristic of David's work in every medium—and of which you cannot say that, being gratuitous, it is unnecessary; for (if the oxymoron may be allowed) it is a beautiful deformity of the very structure. We used to quote among ourselves a saying which we attributed, wrongly I believe, to a French painter, 'There is always something crooked about the beautiful.'[1]

As I wrote that word 'twist', and as my mind considered that peculiar quality, there came back to me with great vividness, the typical gesture with the hands, the twist of the mouth, with which David would struggle to express a similar notion. A delight in good workmanship, which is the starting-point for whatever is represented by that other extra quality, is constantly expressed in David's writing. You see it, too, in his drawing: curl of wrought iron, shaping of stone, texturing of cloth. It crops up in IN PARENTHESIS, even in the middle of that endless, cheerless, first day in the trenches:

'*It was better in the communication trench, where slatters had but lately been at work; and planking, freshly sawn, not yet so walked upon nor mired over, but what its joiner-work could, here and there, make quick that delectation of the mind enjoyed with sight of any common deal, white-pared, newly worked by carpenters. Botched, ill-driven, half-bent-over nail heads protrude, where some transverse piece jointed the lengthways, four-inch under-timber, marking where some*

[1] The source was, probably, much grander, Bacon's sentence: 'There is no excellent beauty that hath not some strangeness in the proportion'.

20

unskilled fatigue-man used his hammer awkwardly, marring the fairness of the thing made—also you trip on the bleeder, very easily.'

In the same autobiographical talk referred to above, David, quoting Sir Ifor Williams, reminds us that

'the bards of an earlier Wales referred to themselves as "carpenters of song".[1] Carpentry suggests a putting together, and as you know the English word "artist" means, at root, someone concerned with a fitting of some sort.'

He might well (as, no doubt, he has done in his mind) have connected that root *ar* with much more—with its frequent appearance in Homer, where (*ararisko*) it is applied to the fitting of helmet to temple, to the mortising of the beams of Odysseus's boat, and so on—and, what is more, with *arma,* implements fitted for defence and offence, implements, too (and primarily) for agriculture: so that Demeter is not only the barley-mother (which seems a reasonable interpretation of her name) but also the mother of man the artificer. Thus, in THE ANATHEMATA we read (p. 230), after a reference to Triptolemus, to whom Demeter taught the arts of agriculture:

> *from dear and grave Demeter come*
> > *germ of all :*
> *of the dear arts as well as bread.*
> *To institute, to make stable*
> *to offer oblations*
> > *permanent*

---

[1] And the Gaulish origin of our word 'carpenter' for 'artificer of wood' must be a delight to David.

> *kindly, acceptable and valid :*
> > *tillage fruit*
> > *man's-norm*
> *then rational*
> > *so food of angels.*

'Dear and grave Demeter'—a lovely rendering, indeed, of the Homeric Hymn's *semnén theon*. As so often happens whenever you quote or read even a few words from David's poetry, you are led down endless side-tracks, which constantly bring you back to the central stream of rite, of offering-up, of adoration. So here Demeter has introduced a digression from the carpentry of song, about which I should have added that, as the Welsh, so the Old Irish poet expresses the same idea when he speaks as a carpenter and prays for help in fitting the pile of timber with which he is struggling. The original eludes me, but a modern version based upon it runs: 'Stone, timber, word-force, sound, tympan, bucina/ will screech-eye [i.e. presumably, Athene] lumber-mix in Mantuan's ordered mine of meaning'.

True artefacture, again, is the theme, carried to a cosmic scale, of THE ANATHEMATA, and in it the Redriff interlude is a eulogy of timber and its proper use. Here David, so far as name, place, and trade were concerned, was in luck (had it, as he says of another passage, *'handed to him on a plate'* for once), in that his maternal grandfather was a mast and block maker, working in Rotherhithe ('Redriff') and named Ebenezer Bradshaw: the perfect name for the main character in that section.

A good deal has been written about Ditchling in the period from 1913 to 1924, and only one thing needs to be added to what has already been said: that no-one except Donald Attwater (in the book quoted earlier) has written about it without exaggeration or distortion. It was a great deal more ordinary, more logical, and less idiosyncratic than many descriptions of it would lead you to believe. The trouble, maybe, was—as is true of Eric himself—that the very normality was an eccentricity. David, anyway, left Ditchling at Christmas 1924 with at least two new acquirements: a knowledge of the art of engraving on wood, which he learnt with the help of Philip Hagreen and Desmond Chute (who was to remain one of his closest friends), and a wider knowledge of the Vulgate to add to the Biblical knowledge that had come to him from his Protestant upbringing.

Just as, in retrospect, all winters brought great drifts of snow, skating and sledging, and all summers seem to have included long tramps over dusty roads in a blaze of sun, so those days at Capel-y-ffin appear as endless talking, in particular about Maritain and the philosophy of art. In fact, for most of the day everyone was busy at work. The greater part of Eric's time was spent in stone-cutting, with one or more assistants, while David was drawing, and engraving the blocks for the Golden Cockerel Press's GULLIVER'S TRAVELS (an uninteresting typographical background to the first engraving job on which his teeth really fastened—an unfortunate expression, I see, now that it is written, for which I apologise: it reminds me of William Morris's reported *'Engrave? Call that*

engraving? I could gnaw better with me teeth'.). From this
time, too, date a number of small end-grain
boxwood carvings, an admirable, accommodat-
ing-to-the-tool material, like ivory, for fine work.
The upper storey of two sides of the monastery
quadrangle was divided into pitch-pine cubicles,
the size of a reasonably large ship's cabin, originally
the cells occupied by Fr. Ignatius's monks. In
these we slept (senior officers, in fact, had proper
bedrooms—I speak of other ranks). It was normal
for whoever was first up in the morning to take
tea aloft to the others. Taking a cup to David one
day, I found him sitting up in bed with a specially
fine example of one of these in his hand, an
elaborate three-figured crucifixion scene, some
three inches square. Handing it to me, he said (as
I thought),

'How would you like that, René?'
'My God! David', I answered, *'what a gift!'*
There was a short silence. Then:
'René, I'm very, very *sorry, but what I said was not how*
would *but how* do *you like it.'*

I wish I knew what happened to that particular
carving. And I digress to tell the story only
because writing it in words gives, for me, a
permanence to the very cherished picture of the
subtle artificer with the anathéma in his hand.

In one respect, however, memory speaks truly:
there can be no doubt about the commanding
position held by Eric and the veneration and
affection he inspired. David well compares him to
William Morris: *'a true master in the sense that Morris was
a master'*. And he was above all a great teacher; both

24

intellectually, in that he gave the pupil a clear, well-defined, uncompromising set of principles (which he could later modify or qualify according to his own intelligence), and in a practical way. The drawing and cutting of the Roman letter is by no means an easily acquired art, but Eric, I do believe, could teach it to literally anyone. (And yet, oddly, he never wrote anything that would help such a pupil—though, on second thoughts, there is nothing odd about that, because the sort of skill he taught could not be drawn from the printed word. It was a matter of workshop practice, and of doing, here and now, this particular thing to this particular material, for this particular purpose.)

It was after supper that most of the talking was done, the unfortunate girls still slaving at sink, stove or spinning-wheel—although the three of them would often sing entrancingly in the evening: Eric, too. The memory of that singing is still with David, and almost any random glance will show how large a part folk-song plays in his poetry. As recently as June 1974 he was writing:

'. . . ask Joan if she could remember the words of that English folk-song that I like best of all, called "The Six Dukes". Eric used to sing it superbly & I knew it by heart till some years back but now only in pieces.
  'I don't often listen to the blasted wireless but a bit back I heard a chap on the "Desert Island Disks" programme which is usually just awful or at best a bit of Bach or other of the "Great Masters". Well, when I was not well in bed a bit back, I turned the bloody thing on & to my astonishment heard with incredulity the heavenly voice of dear Joyce reading that wonderful bit from the end of "Anna Livia" though the brute

had cut it a bit. Then another favourite of mine, a folk Song
(Irish) but can't recall what it was, & then, would you
believe it, "The Six Dukes"—all chosen by the same bloke.
But even that they cut a bit and the bit I like most. The bit
about Six dukes went before him / Six raised him from the
grond / Six dukes followed after him in ther black mourning
gown. Black was their mourning and white was their wand / And
so yellar was the flamboys what they carried in their hond.'

(In fact, David remembered it perfectly, for he then
writes out the text.) 'John Barley-corn' was
another that Eric used to sing, and Barleycorn is
always just round the corner in everything that
David writes.

Often, too, Eric would read to the family (here
the period quality returns). Le Morte D'Arthur
comes specially to mind, with Eric reading the
great story in the second book, of Balin and
Balan: *(O Balin O Balan! / how blood you both / the
Brudersee / toward the last phase / of our dear West.)*
David, of course, had long been familiar with
Malory, ever since as a very small child he had
been given one of the Arthurian stories in the
little paper-covered series (pink, in my memory),
which cost two or three pence, called 'Books for
the Bairns'. Malory was a possession common to
the whole household at Capel, and many of the
Arthurian references and echoes in David's work
must have been maturing in his mind at that
time.

David has used the word 'Socratic' of Eric, and
aptly. He was Socratic in the way in which he
took charge of the conversation, which was
natural enough in view of his seniority (less

pronounced in relation to David than to others of his listeners, for there was only thirteen years difference in their ages), and particularly in his use of a very Socratic irony; he would disguise under the appearance of a mere enquiry or of the acceptance, as a starting-point, of the simplest of dictionary definitions, a mind that was already made up. He proceeded, like Socrates, by question and answer. With Eric is associated the name of Jacques Maritain; and here it is easy to say either too much or too little. Maritain's THE PHILOSOPHY OF ART served as a sort of text-book, but it is easy to attach too much importance to what we learnt from it. In the first place, none of us, except perhaps Dom Theodore Bailey, who for a time shared these conversations, had a real knowledge of the whole system of the Schoolmen; and some professional Thomists might well have seen, and indeed did see, Eric as the devil quoting Scripture —for it is only too easy to select from the ancients what suits your preconceptions and close your eyes to what contradicts them. While, for example, we knew perfectly well that the ancients were indifferent to the distinction between what we call the fine arts and the useful arts, we nevertheless looked to the Schoolmen for a definition of the fine arts, or for a way of accommodating them to the scholastic definition of *ars*. David, we shall see, found a solution to this, or at least found the direction in which the solution lies, and developed a vocabulary in which to express it. It was different with Eric. He was half inclined completely to jettison the fine arts, desperately seeking some 'useful' function for every artefact: David has had to resign himself to accepting the miserable fact that in this culture-less age the artist is necessarily an Ishmael.

'The world of technocracy—and especially its mounting implications suggest the problem's a good deal more difficult, more far-reaching and complex than the problems we used to discuss with Eric and Co. under the head of "industrialism" and "capitalism" etc. The disintegration of "man-the-artist" seems more total and irrevocable than anything we envisaged in those days. I am certain that "man" is "man-the-artist", more certain than ever, but the implications of this become more difficult vis-à-vis the civilisational situation. And, as far as I can see, "man-the-artist" and "man-the-priest" become increasingly, in a sense, Ishmaels, or men of a kind of diaspora, within our technological set-up.'

Writing in 1941, shortly after Eric's death, he has an interesting comment on this matter (EPOCH AND ARTIST, p. 288 f.):

'One need not necessarily subscribe to Spengler's whole thesis to admit that in his "technics instead of lyrics" theme he shows us through which door the wind blows, and that steel wind gathers weight and drive as these unkindly decades proceed. I find it impossible to consider the work of Mr. Gill without keeping in mind this situation, because he sought to work as though a culture of some sort existed or, at all events, he worked as though one should, and could, make a culture exist. Because of his singular qualities as a man he sometimes achieved carvings that looked something like the products of a true culture.'

That last sentence puts its finger upon an important truth. There were occasions when, heaven knows why—some coincidence of time and place, proportion, a chiming of necessity with artistic invention—his 'job to be done' (as

28

it might be shoeing a horse or building an archway) said goodbye to the useful or appropriate and flowered as though upon a true cultural stem—the Westminster Stations of the Cross are an example—and yet the flower still remained strictly 'useful'. Later, in that paper on Eric, David makes a remark which adds some explanation to what was said earlier about the peculiar 'twist' in the beautiful: Eric, he says, *'so to say, attacked frontally'*.

Another point to be borne in mind in connection with Maritain is that the 1920's in England (following France) marked the height of the neo-Thomist revival. It was, moreover, a time when 'Catholic' was used in a narrower sense than it bears now: so that with Catholicism and scholasticism a certain evangelism was associated, as though one were preaching the only gospel that could be accepted. It was the time, too, when Teilhard de Chardin was being silenced for his evolutionary views, and was finding that terms derived from a static Aristotelian and Thomistic view of the universe could not be used to express his own cosmology, and in particular his view of spirit as the inevitable product of the growing complexity of matter. This had hardly as yet percolated through to English Catholic circles. We lacked an infusion of existentialism, even of Marxism, in that sense of both which sees man as the maker of his own being, so that he and his works cannot be pinned down and analysed, cannot be treated as 'stills' from a moving picture. Eric never used the word alienation, although it expresses the idea that was so often in his mind. David speaks at least once of *'man's alienation from his*

poiesis'. This is not a suggestion that David is
Marxist where Eric was not: but simply that Eric
insisted on 'technical' alienation, David on
'poietic'.

While too much, then, should not be attributed
to Maritain's influence, it should not, on the other
be minimised; for the cut and dried approach to
the problems of artefacture had this advantage,
that something hard, sharp and definite could be
grasped and qualified later. The two men reacted
very differently to that elementary training. In
spite of his ceaseless defence of the claims of art
against prudence, Eric was very much a man of
prudence (David, again, has a nice phrase here:
'Prudence is a great hustler'). He looked at the problem
from the point of view of his own self with a
family (and often with more than a family) to
maintain while at the same time retaining his
human dignity as a creator; but he looked at it,
too, not from the point of view of the 'artist'—
who, God help him, cannot be other than such—
but from that of the ordinary working man
robbed by industrialism of that same dignity and
faced with the same difficulty. Eric was a tireless
would-be social reformer. If I may be pardoned
for obtruding my own self, I have printed so much
of Eric's work that were I now—though it is
nearly twenty years since I savoured the smell of
printers' ink—standing at the composing-frame,
stick in hand, my hands would almost auto-
matically travel around the case picking out the
sorts which would form the sentence (quoted by
Eric, so often, from Fr. Martin D'Arcy) *'Industrialism
has reduced the workman to a subhuman condition of intellectual
irresponsibility'*. Eric was concerned with the

scandal that men were denied that virtue which was defined by our old friend *recta ratio factibilium.* David was more concerned with the real 'artificer's' position in that scandalous civilisation. He added a great deal, largely from his reading of Maurice de la Taille, to that key phrase, as can be seen in his much-quoted essay, 'Art and Sacrament', in EPOCH AND ARTIST. The way in which he developed it, and the width of his interpretation, appear again at the very beginning of THE ANATHEMATA, in its elevation into *adscriptam, ratam, rationabilem,* with the accompanying note—though I never read that note without wishing that David had included the Finberg-O'Connell translation (published only a short time before a reference to the 'Roman Mass' became an anachronism) '. . . wholly blessed, a thing consecrated and approved, worthy of the human spirit and of thy acceptance'. Here *rationabilis* and *recta ratio* are taken to the scale of creation and applied to the supreme act of creation, the oblation of self to self ineluctably bound up with the immolation of self—the supremely gratuitous.

It is in their lettering that the difference between Eric and David is most apparent. Here Eric, the supreme master of clarity and restraint, was truly classic, in the strict sense of conforming to norm. He never imposed the strict Roman form on David; there are just a few pieces of David's lettering dating from the Ditchling period in which he evidently has been at pains not to depart from Eric's standard, but even in these the romantic (or, since David is somewhat wary of that dangerous word, what he has called the 'associative-romantic') keeps breaking in. This can be seen also at Capel-y-ffin, where David painted a crucifix, with a fairly long inscription, on the wall of Eric's stone-workshop, and in the tabernacle for the chapel at Capel, the painted door of which is reproduced in the 1967 David Jones issue of AGENDA. Later, these departures have been carried much further. Eric would have been speechless had a pupil drawn those R's whose tails unblushingly thrust themselves from the junction of bow and stem, the slender S's that look to their neighbour, or to the margin, for support, the G's whose variety is an essay in calligraphic development, the E's that so craftily combine squareness with rotundity, the whole effect of an inscription—like a logan stone which the touch of a hand will rock and which yet stands solid and unmoving. Where did all these forms come from? They did not originate, as did Eric's, from asking, *'What constitutes an A?'* but from the same sources as the imagery of David's poetry, and it would take a deal of learning to trace them back, just as it does to trace back the verbal juxtapositions in the poems. The remarkable thing about David's inscriptional work is that there is in it nothing that is purely fanciful; every shape is determined by the particular evocation required in *this* place for *this* thought. There is nothing of the licence which makes the lettering of art nouveau and the nineties so foolish, nothing, on the other hand, standardised; there is no antiquarianism, but a great deal of scholarship, a knowledge of, and contribution to, tradition. Here, indeed, the *recta ratio* takes some chasing, and here the welding of form and content assumes an even fuller meaning: as in a poem which, like 'Cloelia, Cornelia, with the

Palmyrene . . .' (also reproduced in the AGENDA issue), is inseparable from the inscription. It has the fulness of its existence only in the one original object. Compare such work with the august elegance of Eric's incised or engraved letters, and you see how different an interpretation *recta ratio* can bear. In David's case it produces a mine of allusion, suggestion, remembrance; in Eric's sheer purity of form. David notes (EPOCH AND ARTIST, p. 300 f.), when speaking of Eric as a letter-cutter:

'As a carver of inscriptions he stands supreme. There the workman scaled the heights of pure form, and some of his inscribed stones possess that anonymous and inevitable quality we associate with the works of the great civilisations, where an almost frightening technical skill, for a rare moment, is the free instrument of the highest sensitivity—and the Word is made Stone.'

To revert, however, to Maritain and Eric's views on industrialism and the arts: we spend a good deal of our time in this twilight of our culture in reading books about books rather than the books themselves. There are not many who would care to extract a philosophy directly from Aristotle, Albert and Aquinas, and not very many more, probably, who would care to read even Maritain. Gill is easy enough to read, in all conscience, but some may find him too repetitive and too anxious continually to ram home his point. The reader who wishes to understand Eric and his influence on David, and to understand, too, what is contained in the great classical tradition which, for our purpose, led up to Aquinas, should read a couple of short essays in Walter Shewring's

Making and Thinking[1], 'Art in Christian Philosophy' and 'Considerations on Eric Gill'. He writes the first from a much wider knowledge of classical philosophy than Eric possessed, and in the second he sets Eric's views in a much wider cultural perspective. He is eminently clear and succinct, and the carefully chosen illustrations are a powerful reinforcement to his argument. His treatment, in particular, of the useful arts and fine arts division is most persuasive; and he approaches from a different angle a subject that has always been of prime importance to David, the distinction between culture and civilisation. It is from Walter Shewring that I borrow a comparison which illuminates what David means by the 'utile' and the 'extra-utile', the rationally deduced and the gratuitous, the technical and the pure. When you look at Brancusi's 'Bird in Space' and the harpoon head, approximately the same shape, from the Marquesas Islands (both are illustrated in the book mentioned above), you will be hard put to it to decide which of the two has the greater extra-utile quality. It is in commenting on these two that Walter Shewring, after pointing out that *viewed as a shaped and patterned thing, it (the harpoon) has the same subtleties, the same appeal and implications, as Brancusi's 'pure sculpture'*, reminds us of Lethaby's remark, *'artificer and artist seem to be two forms of the same word. One has gone up in the world, the other down. Which is which?'* But however that question is answered, to the harpoon, as to a number of 'useful' objects David himself has made, we must give praise for being (in words taken from, and with the weight of the context of, 'The Kensington

---

[1] The Catholic Art Association, Buffalo, New York, 1968.

Mass') *straight, exact, rational and true.* One more quotation I must borrow from the same source, which is a fine start for meditation and a pithy summary of Eric's thought, Lethaby's *Art must be everywhere. It cannot exist in isolation, or only one man thick. It must be a thousand men thick.*

III

The Great War and 'In Parenthesis'

In a letter quoted earlier, David speaks of the first
beginnings of IN PARENTHESIS; another letter, dated
September 1963, gives the date of completion. A
packet containing the copy from which the type
was set had come to him, unexpectedly, by post:

*'It tells me an interesting thing that I was very surprised about.
At the conclusion of Part VII it says "finished at Pigotts,
18th August 1932". The notes and preface were written
mainly at Sidmouth in 1935—that I knew, but I thought I did
bits of the text between 1932 and 1935. However, that's what it
says. Do you remember our going in 1936 to see Richard de la
Mare and wondering if they [Fabers] could be persuaded to print
the thing in long columns like a newspaper, in "Joanna"
type-face? What a hope!'*

It was thus, in fact that the first specimen pages of
IN PARENTHESIS were printed. The publisher's
consternation was remarkable, and a less unusual
presentation was finally accepted. These proofs
were pulled on a type of Cope's Albion hand-
press which is seldom seen; it is the subject of
David's watercolour drawing 'Hague's Press'
which is reproduced in colour in the little
Penguin Painters book referred to earlier. By the
time the book was ready for press, we had moved
our printing works to High Wycombe from
Pigotts, and it was machined on a fairly large
modern machine. To the best of my recollection,
the first impression was of 1,500 copies, followed

a few months later by a second impression of, I think, 1,000 copies: a trifling number to be sold of a book which was received with immediate astonished praise on all sides, and has since been the subject of so much study and explanation.

IN PARENTHESIS is one of several books which appeared from about 1929 onwards, all concerned with the battle of the Somme (1st July 1916), written by men who served in that battle, or rather offensive, with the Royal Welch Fusiliers: Robert Graves's GOODBYE TO ALL THAT (the relevant part, that is, of Graves's book), Llywelyn Wyn Griffith's UP TO MAMETZ, Frank Richards's OLD SOLDIERS NEVER DIE, Siegfried Sassoon's MEMOIRS OF AN INFANTRY OFFICER. These were books which David had read at that time and of which he frequently spoke. He had been turning over in his mind the possibility of some sort of writing before he read any of these, but he must have read them fairly soon after their publication; and there can be little doubt that Graves, in particular, parts of whose book spoke directly to David, must have acted as some sort of prompter. The general pattern followed in GOODBYE TO ALL THAT, is, as a matter of historical, not literary, fact, very similar to that followed by IN PARENTHESIS, and the passage in Graves's book which describes the first move up to the front line has a great deal in common (the terrain, the trench-system) with Part 3 of IN PARENTHESIS. Frank Richard's book is a most interesting marginal comment on David's, because it is written by a private soldier, a reservist, one who completely accepts soldiering as any tradesman accepts his craft: written, in fact, as though by one of the characters in IN

PARENTHESIS. The relation of IN PARENTHESIS to those mentioned above has been studied by William Blissett in his paper 'IN PARENTHESIS among the war-books'[1]—glancing at which reminds me of the Jesuit Fr. Richard Steuart's MARCH, KIND COMRADE. The publisher gave this a link with David: the Hopkins title, and the drawing which David made as frontispiece.

The first question asked by any newcomer to IN PARENTHESIS is 'What is it about?', and the question can be answered simply enough (the preceding paragraph, in fact, is a sufficient answer), but the answer will say nothing about what the book is. Reading the quotation on the title-page, the dedication and the passage from the Mabinogion which follows it, with the appropriate notes, one might attempt to define IN PARENTHESIS as a poetic transmutation of personal experience into a memorial to, and a lament for, the ancient unity of this island of Britain. A further point: each of the seven parts is preceded by an epigraph taken from the sixth-century Welsh poem Y GODODDIN, which is concerned with a Welsh raid from what we would call Edinburgh to Saxon-held Catraeth (Catterick, in Yorkshire?). Three hundred horsemen were concerned, of whom but three survived. With the Somme offensive in mind, however, we should remember that when the mob of infantry is included (as neglected in Welsh epic as in Homer) this was a considerable force. And, remembering the sequence of events in IN PARENTHESIS, we should note the relevance of each epigraph,

---

[1] UNIVERSITY OF TORONTO QUARTERLY, 42 (3) 1973.

setting the tone, as it were, of the modern piece. Thus, part one, the march to the port of embarkation: *'Men marched, they kept equal step . . .'*; part six, the assembly-point before the attack on 10th July: *'Men went to Catraeth . . . death's sure meeting-place, the place of their gathering'*; part seven, the attack, when *'sweet sister death . . . stalks on this high ground': 'Gododdin I demand thy support . . .'* (for one reader at least this is a poignant looking forward to the opening cry of a later desperate poem, *A, a, a, Domine Deus*) . . . *'It is our duty to sing'*.

The manner of the writing came as a shock to readers in 1937, bringing as much bewilderment as delight; but there seems to be a common fund of understanding which grows with time, and fifteen years later, when THE ANATHEMATA produced a similar bewilderment, IN PARENTHESIS had lost most of its difficulty. Critics looked to other writers for a clue to David's method. This is his own comment:

'Someone, the other day, said to me something to the effect that in I.P. he supposed I had deeply studied the techniques used in Ulysses, that this was evident from the switch from observed concrete outward actions and things to the interior "dream-like" colloquies of the characters. I told him that I had not read Ulysses, either before, during or since writing I.P. and that I have still not read it; which is no doubt regrettable but true . . . you had read aloud to Joan and myself some part of that separately published bit of ANNA LIVIA, but that was certainly after 1938 and may have been round about 1930[1]— cant recall. From time to time since 1948 (note in margin of the letter: but only from time to time and latterly not much. And

---

[1] It must, in fact, have been 1930 or 1931.

during the actual writing of THE ANATHEMATA *I deliberately did not read Joyce or Pound or other "contemporary" writers—for one thing I had such a lot of other stuff, "sources" etc. to check up on: might have been Welsh stuff or Caesar or Gregory of Nyssa or what not) I've struggled with bits of* FINNEGAN'S WAKE *and though its taken me always some hours to "understand" any given paragraph I've always found it astounding in the many, many, facetted evocations of each word or group of words, and* usually, *or very often, gloriously amusing into the bargain, not to mention the very great pulchritude shining out from the juxtaposed forms; . . . But as for the* usual talk *of influences, hell's bells, it's boring.'*

On the other hand, when a person first sets out to fit words together, the tools at his disposal and the method of using them must first come from what he has absorbed: the mere style of the writing, that is to say, the range of vocabulary, the structure of the sentence. There is a curious, quiet, little interval of rest and conversation with two friends in part six (pp. 139-40)

—'*These three loved one another, but the routine of their lives made chance for gathering rare.*'

Discussing books, they mention, naturally enough, H. G. Wells and Rupert Brooke. But tucked away on page 78 (with a note attached) is a reference to Hilaire Belloc. Now, David is a man easily moved to delighted amusement, and passionately devoted to the exactly ordered, including the precise, deliberate arrangement of simple words. This he found in Belloc: the Belloc of THE EYE-WITNESS, THE FRENCH REVOLUTION and MARIE ANTOINETTE—a man, there, of great artistry, in spite of his over-rigid views on the arts. He wrote with a studied, almost artificial simplicity that only the most ill-natured critic would regard as affectation. He had, too, a romanticism shared by David. He would use 'Gaul' as David would use it now, with the same resonance. Two passages as illustration come to mind, both of precisely the kind in which David delights. The first is from an essay on 'The servants of the rich':

These are those who would take the tattered garments [of the Poor Guest] and hold them at arm's length as much as to say: 'What rags these scribblers wear!' and then, casting them over the arm with a gesture that meant: 'Well, they must be brushed, but Heaven knows if they will stand it without coming to pieces', would next discover in the pockets a great quantity of middle-class things, and notably loose tobacco . . . 'What a jumble these paupers stuff their shoddy with'.

I suppose David has shared more laughter with his friends over those sentences than over anything else except the Grossmiths' Pooter or Hamish Maclaren's William Taplow—and Taplow certainly left his mark (recognisable though not generally recognised) on IN PARENTHESIS.

The second passage is from Belloc's MARIE ANTOINETTE, and occurs in his account of the attack, as the mist lifted, on Wattignies (16th-17th October 1793):

The 16th of October broke upon the Flemish hills: the men who had endured that night-march along the front of the battle-field, the men who had received them among the positions of the extreme right, still drooped under the growing light and were invigorated by no sun. The mist of the evening and of the night from dripping and thin had grown dense and whitened with the

41

morning, so that to every soldier a new despair and a new bewilderment were added from the very air, and the blind fog seemed to make yet more obscure the obscure designs of their commanders. The day of their unnatural vigil had dawned, and yet there came no orders nor any stirring of men. Before them slow schistous slopes went upwards and disappeared into the impenetrable weather which hid clogged ploughland and drenched brushwood of the rounded hill; hollow lanes led up through such a land to the summit of the little rise and the hamlet of Wattignies; this most humble and least of villages was waiting its turn for glory.

It is surely not fanciful to see in that writing a kinship with narrative passages in IN PARENTHESIS: the bringing together, in sharp focus, of soldiers and landscape, the careful use of adjective, and, most characteristically, that one, slightly odd, semi-technical word 'schistous' which conveys the exact nature of the terrain. Belloc, of course, never wrote with the obliquity with which David approaches his work, but David owes him some considerable debt in the structure of his sentences. There used to be in existence a delightful sketch, symbolic of David's amused pleasure in the man, in which David has drawn Belloc sitting, cigarette in hand, smoke curling upwards, under a large 'No Smoking' notice: Belloc, at the time was taking the chair at a debate in the Essex Hall between Chesterton and Shaw.

Here, too (not for style, but for matter and method) is a convenient place to remember Coleridge. David has always been interested in the working of the poetic mind, and has written a good deal about it—a very useful by-product of his writing being that it illuminates his own work

42

as much as, or even more than, that of the poet he
is considering. He read with great interest, most
probably soon after its publication in 1927, and
often spoke about, Livingston Lowes's ROAD TO
XANADU; and this examination of the mechanics
of the poet's imagination must surely have
suggested to him, even if he was not consciously
aware of the suggestion, the *sort* of lines on which
work could be done. Coleridge, moreover, was
much in David's mind at this time, for the
Douglas Cleverdon edition of the ANCIENT
MARINER, with David's copper-engravings, was
published in 1929, and he had been working on
the plates for some time. He says that, round
about 1928, he made *'between 150 and 200 pencil drawings
for the ten plates'*. In Coleridge, David could see at
work what the former calls by the barbarous but
useful name of the 'esemplastic' process of
imagination, the moulding into one (that is, into
real being) of matter stored away. Coleridge
has been with David all his life, and forty-five
years after reading Livingston Lowes—when the
ANCIENT MARINER was re-published, again with
David's plates—he wrote a long introduction in
which he develops the thesis he finds in Coleridge
(as in a good deal of ancient literature) and has
used in his own work: the journey of the human
soul as an odyssey, of man as the argonaut, and
(carrying the idea into what is most dear to him)
of Christ himself as the supreme thalassic voyager.
This theme was later to run through THE
ANATHEMATA, in the voyaging from the Mediterranean, the passage up-channel and up the North
Sea, the re-fit at Rotherhithe, and finally the end
of the redeemer's voyage in the 'Keel, Ram,
Stauros' section. One passage at least should be

quoted, for this Introduction was published in a limited edition not available to many readers, a companion volume to the second printing of the ANCIENT MARINER itself.[1]

'. . . *in the long run and certainly for us to-day it is impossible not to see the validity and rightness of Gregory of Nazianzus, of Basil of Caesarea, of Gregory of Nyssa, of Clement of Alexandria, of Ambrose of Milan and of various other less known figures in perceiving that much in the Odysseus saga (and other Classical deposits) had correspondences in the voyaging of the Christian soul and in the argosy of the Son of God.*

The 4th century patristic writers . . . saw amidships the image of the same salvific Wood. And not the yarded mast only, but the planking and timbers composing the vessel, so of the chief timber, the Keel.

It was this idea of the keel that I tried specially to convey in one section of THE ANATHEMATA, *section VI, "Keel, Ram, Stauros"; in section IV, "Redriff", the mast especially, and in other sections, the ship and the voyage.'*

And, reverting again to the 'carpentry of song' and David's delight in the aptly fashioned and the technically exact, we find him at the end of the next paragraph quoting the 'strictly factual' nautical definition of the keel as 'Principal member of a ship's construction'. This long essay ends with a couple of sentences which illustrate the light which David sheds on his own work when writing of another poet. He is explaining the engraved tail-piece, which represents the pelican feeding her young, with the inscription 'Accendat in nobis . . .', and he ends:

---

[1] By Clover Hill Editions, London, 1972.

'*May the Lord kindle in us the fire of his love and the flame of eternal charity. Words which seemed to tally with the third stanza from the end of the poem, and which express a theme that runs like a thread through the whole mysterious weft and warp of* THE RIME OF THE ANCIENT MARINER.' And in those sentences it is not only the theme that comes to mind as being applicable to the whole body of David's work, but also the notion of *texture,* the intricate weaving into a whole fabric.

Milton, too, this Introduction reminds us, lies close behind Coleridge: again a life-long companion, for David's father would always, on Christmas morning, read to his family the hymn 'On the morning of Christ's nativity'. Here again David comments on Milton's use of *'the analogy taken from a ship's essential wood',* felled and fit *'to be the Mast of some great Ammiral',* introducing it for the sake of the contrast between the image representing the *'Dreaming Tree that bore up the young hero that waes god aelmihtig'* and *'the colossal spearhaft in the supposed almighty fist-grip of his* [Milton's] *god-damned Lucifer'.*

So much has been written about IN PARENTHESIS, that what follows is not an attempt at further description but rather by way of marginal annotation. David has described parts of the book, particularly in the earlier sections, as almost straightforward reporting. This is not strictly true, for even in the most commonplace communications there is always something in his use of words which flows over into poetry. (It is true, however, that the intensity of the writing increases gradually, which is a help to the inexperienced reader—who should, even so, watch his step from the very first line.) It is interesting, then, to compare (with David's permission) a factual account of his movements with the finished language of IN PARENTHESIS. The following, for example, from a letter of July 1973, describes among other things the march to the port of embarkation (Part one) and later the march from the La Bassée sector to the Somme (Part five):

'I at first tried hard to recall a specific day—the day very early in the morning we paraded in our camp parade ground on a hill outside Winchester (Winnol Down, I think it is called) and then found I could remember quite a bit about the march in the driving rain to Southampton, & waiting in some sort of very large shed & embarking in the drizzle in the vessel that took us to the mouth of the Seine. It was by painfully trying to remember some specific thing or event or what not in chrono-logical order backwards (not necessarily sticking to that chronology) that I found things slowly came to mind—for example the sodden field & our first billets in France as described in the opening pages of Part two is practically straight "reportage"—we were there for about a fortnight or over. I have no maps, damnation! with me here or I could point out with some exactitude where we were . . . Anyway gradually by getting a clear picture of some given situation I could then recall another bit further back or rather further forward and slowly by trying to recall what happened at such & such a time, was able to join the established points, but it was rather like a map of e.g. the Roman viae . . . Parts 3 & 4 are virtually a pretty exact chronicle. Part 5 uses remembered things as "materia poetica" covering a number of months from say January 1916 to May or June 1916. All is of events in the same sector & the routine was repeated but we sometimes would be in one part of that sector—say on the Richebourg-Neuve Chapelle bit or in the bit south of that, in the Givenchy area & that never to be forgot place of a tangle of trenches, so close were his trenches to ours, and in places not only close but seemed to be intermeddled with each other. I have never seen an aerial photograph of the place, but that is what it felt like. No fires by day because of smoke, and no fires by night because of the gleam giving the position away—those at least were the orders but somehow or other we managed & so did he. Occasionally some idiot would discharge a rifle-grenade, which always meant retaliation, most likely from a light trench-mortar. The "no-man's land" between the opposed forces was in places a solid briary brake of red rusted entanglement of wire. The place was also undermined and countermined. "The concavities of it is not sufficient for look you th' adversary . . . is digt himself four yard under the countermines: by Cheshu, a' will plow all up, if there is not better directions". It was from this bit of frontage that when we were relieved we came back along the tow-path of a canal that marked the line of division between the Givenchy sector and that of Cuinchy (in I.P. p.116 Guinchy is, I think, wrong; it should be Cuinchy) which was equally horrible, I'm told. Anyway no wonder I speak with affection of green "Gorre of the sheltering coppice"— It was a strange little place with some kind of dredging machinery—but for some unknown reason never shelled though it was within easy range of Jerry's guns. I find I say in I.P. "when you come from the Islands" here "Islands" refer to separate posts a bit north of Givenchy—on the Festubert front, "Festering Hubert" in our lingo. Anway Part 5 has nothing in it that was not actually experienced, but unlike most of the other parts telescopes the routine of going into the front line & reserve line & occasional periods in the Forward Reserve Area —Divisional baths etc.

David then goes on to discuss an 'admirable, deeply sympathetic' paper by Tom Dilworth[1] on

---

[1] In the same issue of the University of Toronto Quarterly as that referred to above.

'The Parenthetical Liturgy of David Jones', which includes a typically Davidian comment. Speaking of the vagueness of the word 'mystic' he says that it is

'not indeed quite as bad as the word myth, for that is about the limit in loss of meaning. The Shorter Oxford Dictionary, 1936 edn, the only Dict. I have here, starts off in defining "myth" as (i) "a purely fictitious narrative", a bloody lie, in fact.'

It is in this connection that he continues, in a passage which is quoted here as an illumination of IN PARENTHESIS but which has even more force as a comment on THE ANATHEMATA:

'. . . I merely wished to indicate that in writing "In. Paren." I had no intention whatever in presuming to compare the varied maims, death-strokes, miseries, acts of courage etc. of the two contending forces, ours or "those against whom we found ourselves by misadventure" with the Passion, Self-Oblation & subsequent Immolation & death of the cult-hero of our Xtian tradition for that is a unique and profound Mystery of Faith. He, by whom all things are that are, Deum de Deo, Deum verum de Deo vero, "placed himself in the order of signs" and under the signum *of actual real, substantial mortal flesh, of the flesh of Mair, the* fiat-*giver,* ceidwades Wen et Mundi Domina in Liknites *cave was seen of the herdsmen wrapped in swaddlings* in praesepio *and over thirty years later—with his chosen* turba *seated, himself the offerent and the victim, made the Oblation that committed him inescapably to the bloody Immolation at the hands of others. If this is not a* mysterium *and a true* mythos, *what could it be?'*

Speaking then of his gratitude to the Canadian scholar for using *'his water-diviner's rod with such accuracy'* in many details, David quotes the corporal's doling out of the rations including the rum ration (pp. 73-4):

'*Well, he, Tom D., was quite right in seeing that the words used recalled the cruse of oil of a widow of Sarephta and Elias's miraculous action in regard to it . . . and in seeing that the whole episode of doling out the rations is told in such a way that betrays the author's unconscious use of terms such as "and this is thank-worthy" and carrying with careful fingers their own daily bread. But only very remotely did I think of this sacral distribution, I was merely recalling a vivid remembrance of another repeated scene & the very positive protest if it looked as though some over-anxious jolting might spill the small-enough ration. I can see the longish iron ladle now which was used sometimes when there was a poor issue. Usually we were allowed to put the stuff into our mess-tin covers . . . it fitted perfectly with that lanky corporal with his "longe ladel" of Chaucer's cook.'*

Earlier in this same letter David speaks of the march south and the arrival (Part 6) at the 'terrain of bivouac':

'*Since 1st July my thoughts have continuously returned to what I was doing* in illo tempore *57 years ago. I could not remember with any exactitude where we were on any given day —on that southward trek from the La Bassée front to the chalk lands of the Somme area, but reveille each day was very early (about 3.30 a.m. as far as I can recall it) so as to march as far as possible in the less hot parts of the day. With those who had gone sick because of blistered feet starting earlier still—there was no other way for there were no vehicles available for hobbling men. But to-day 9th July we had somehow arrived and were in the field of bivouac I suppose, as described in Part 6 of I.P. Tomorrow 10th July between 3 a.m. and 4 a.m. we were* on the western slope of the "high embankment" of page 154 of I.P. called on English trench maps "Queen's Nullah" very appropriate a name for the C.O. and his friend to chat awhile of their days in India—where "Colonel Dell presumed to welcome" one of his old friends from Poona days.'

And, to conclude, an annotation to the end of Part 7:

'Talking of "mass" and what the scientists tell us of velocity causing weight—I suppose that's why when a machine-gun or maybe rifle bullet passed clean through my left leg without touching the fibula or tibia—but merely through the calf, it felt as if a great baulk of timber or a heavy bar of some sort had struck me sideways, in fact I thought a ponderous branch had been severed by shrapnel and had fallen across my leg but couldn't account for the extreme violence and weight. I did not realise it was S.A.A. until I tried to stand up & felt the wetness seeping from the wound that I'd been hit by a mere little bullet, but the disproportion of the smallness of the nickel projectile and the great bludgeoning weight of the impact astonished me even at the time.'

IV

'The Anathemata' and the sacramental

Before turning to THE ANATHEMATA, *'the one'*, in David's words, *'that really matters'*, there are two small incidents from his spell of garrison duty in Limerick which should be recorded. The military authorities thought that battle-tried troops needed a fresh infusion of bull and savagery, and this included an 'assault course'. Going through this, David sprained his ankle badly, and the M.O. had given him a stick to help him get about. Hobbling around the parade-ground, he was spotted by the R.S.M. In commiserating with a friend who had also sprained her ankle, David writes:

'At least you wont have to hear our R.S.M. Jones, being a man subject to authority and saying three times "Put that stick down." "No, sir: the M.O. gave it to me." "Put that bloody stick down." "No, sir." "Put that stick down." "No, sir." "Very well: fall out yous two men" (note in margin: I've never discovered why, but so often "yous two", in place of "you two" was employed—especially by Scots N.C.O.s, but this beauty was a Londoner, not a Scot) "fix bay'nets—At the slope if you dont mind, and escort this man to the guard room. Tell the sergeant of the guard to put this man under close arrest." '

In retrospect, David is astonished that so experienced a soldier should have been so impossibly rash—but exasperation overcame prudence. He was, in the event, fortunate enough to have the extremely grave charge of 'refusing three times' to obey an order—while on active service— reduced to 'hesitating to obey'. The story illustrates what is lacking to the basic truth expressed in *'the artist is not a special kind of man; every man is a special kind of artist'* : that within the class *'special kind of artist'* there are artificers, the true poets in particular, whose whole life is so ordered to their artefacture that life itself is their material. So here the R.S.M.'s words and the tone in which they were spoken have been stored up—to re-appear on more than one occasion. They give a special bite to the N.C.O.'s sarcasm in *'The Fatigue'*

> *Mind that step*
> *the leading file*
> *this is the Procurator of Judaea's night relief*
> *stepping the smooth-laid silex of the wall*
> *not the radiant Cymbeline's*
> *trousered Catuvellauni*
> *having a cut at*
> *the* passus Romanus
> *pick 'em up in front*
> *Keep that regulation step.*

Between the maximum and minimum of the extra-utile there are endless degrees, and, as we know from countless other experiences, a difference of degree can ultimately produce a difference of kind. It is in this sense that we may interpret the apparent paradox in the last sentence of the opening quotation from Harman Grisewood; *'had he never put brush or pen to paper, he would have led the life of an artist in himself'*.

The second passage is re-quoted from a piece in

AGENDA[1] (to which, in fact, what is written here is a commentary), for the same reason as the first, and also because it is itself so beautiful a composition, with the final words showing what is a combination of the pre- and post-Vergilian David. The fusiliers were returning to barracks from a route-march:

'It was a red sundown and I was coming with some other Fusiliers along a wet hill-road by a whitewashed cabin and we met a girl with a torn white shift of sorts with a red skirt with a plum-coloured hem to the skirt which reached a bit below the knee; and she had auburn hair floating free over her shoulders and in the wind, and her feet and arms were bare and she had a long stick; she was driving a red-coloured cow before her and the evening sun bathed all these differing reds and bronzes . . . For some reason that's another image I associate with Troy— the red sunset on the red cattle-girl in Munster . . . cattle raiders, horse raiders, soldiers, queens, queans, and the red as of flame—and the great dignity—well, fuit Ilium.'

That last fragment is a fine introduction to THE ANATHEMATA, to the poet himself, to his method, his type of association and imagery, his sense of dignity, pathos, oneness. But how does one describe the poem to a person who comes to it as a complete stranger and again asks the dual question, what is it *about* and what does it *contain*? The answer to the first half is given in the title. It is about the anathemata, and what that means we are told in the preface (pp. 27-9). After discussing the meanings of the word and the distinction between the two cognate words *ana'thema* and *anathe'ma,* David continues:

---

[1] The David Jones issue mentioned earlier.

'*So I mean by my title as much as it can be made to mean, or can evoke or suggest, however obliquely: the blessed things that have taken on what is cursed and the profane things that somehow are redeemed: the delights and also the "ornaments", both in the primary sense of gear and paraphernalia and in the sense of what simply adorns; the donated and votive things, the things dedicated after whatever fashion, the things in some sense made separate, being "laid up from other things"; things, or some aspect of them that partake of the extra-utile and of the gratuitous; things that are the signs of something other, together with those signs that not only have the nature of a sign, but are themselves, under some mode, what they signify. Things set up, lifted up, or in whatever manner made over to the gods.*'

To this we may append a note from Maritain:

'. . . *this is why art, inasmuch as it is ordered to beauty, does not, at least when its object permits, stop at forms or colours, nor at sounds, nor at words taken in themselves and* as things *(though this is how they must necessarily be taken in the first place) but it takes them* also *as making known other things than themselves, that is to say* as signs. *And the thing signified may itself be a sign in turn, and the more the work of art is laden with significance (but spontaneous and intuitively grasped, not hieroglyphic significance), the vaster and the richer and the higher will be the possibility of joy and beauty.*'

So that we may say that THE ANATHEMATA is about the making of signs, about man as sign-maker, and above all, about the incarnate God as the supreme sign-maker. It is 'about' precisely what it both opens with, and closes with, the sacrifice of the Mass. It is here that de la Taille is added to Maritain, and a sentence from the

former might well serve as an epigraph to THE
ANATHEMATA:

*To the God who gave him all, man gives himself whole and
entire. And that he may be acceptable to God, man prays:
he prays that God may draw to himself what comes to us from
him, and that God may keep to himself what has been
consecrated to him,* Latria, *eucharist, impetration (adoration,
thanksgiving, petition) go side by side and hand in hand in this
first approach of man to God.*

   *But because man is not a pure spirit, he feels a need to
translate this interior gift of himself into an outward rite which
symbolizes it. For this reason he presents to God the homage of
some material gift, the whole reason and purpose of which is to
represent and attest the inmost consecration of his soul.*

And so we are brought back again to the opening
of THE ANATHEMATA: *adscriptam, ratam, rationabilem.*
And looking back at the Demeter passage quoted
earlier, we can see that that, too, sums up the
theme of THE ANATHEMATA.

David has explained at some length in his EPOCH
AND ARTIST what he means by the sacramental,
and the impossibility of separating artefacture
from man's nature as a sign-making creature:
there is a passage in 'Art and Sacrament' (pp.
168 ff.) which puts his view with special force and
clarity; in this he explains how '*the truth that Ars is
inalienable from Man and Man from Ars*' must impose
itself both upon non-Christian and upon
Christian, but how, also, it is only the latter who
can see in the act of Ars that took place 'in the
supper room', 'an *unique,* most compelling and
ratifying example' of that truth—as opposed to
merely 'a further example'. He then goes on to

tell how he found, as an art-student in 1919, that post-impressionist theory could lead into, and be accommodated to that truth—and of the difficulty in getting this understood. He adds, in a letter, many years later (1972) than those youthful discussions:

'Yes, the Maritain part . . . but they never get that right. When I was at Westminster Art School in 1919-20 before I'd ever heard of Maritain etc. I used to say to chaps that I thought the theory of Post-impressionism, about painting and what not being a thing and not the impression of some thing, was analogous to what the Catholic Church maintained in her dogma of the Mass—they thought I was cracked (especially the Catholic ones!). Well, since those days I've tried a fair number of times—but no, they wont bite. I was "inside" a Catholic in the trenches in 1917, but not so formally until 1921.'

I cannot refrain from quoting two more similar extracts from letters, which bear upon the same point and illustrate the conversion of thesis into poetic form: for they can be seen as intermediate between the conception of the notion of the sign and the actualising of the sign in (in this instance) THE ANATHEMATA:

'It is foolish, so it seems to me, to pretend that the Catholic mythus is other than a complex of mysteries of inexplicable splendour, that is consonant with man as a sign-making animal. The Roman liturgy, as it stood with the chant, was a stupendous art-work loaded with the sacral, apperceived not by the understanding of this or that particular word or words but by the whole of man's faculties—as inutile as Mary Maudlin's precious unguents poured out from the fractured alabaster, a reprehensible act of the most inutile sort—but the Cult-hero gave a sharp reponse to those of that opinion, "Let her be, I tell

56

you straight that wherever in the whole world is sung the chanson of my deeds this shall be told in anamnesis of her." She surely is the tutelar of the extra-utile that covers all Ars and all religio other than what is sometimes called "practical religion".'

Argument, there, begins to move into poetry, and clarifies the oneness, so hard to define, of arte-facture and adoration. Later, in the same letter, David describes his first sight of a mass: and this, I believe, illustrates better than any comment from outside the nature of his artistry, the gathering of the material and its transmutation into some thing which shows forth another more tremendous thing:

'It was after the Somme, I think, so when I had returned to France from being wounded—Anyway when or where it was I cannot exactly place. But as I was always cold, one of my main occupations was to hunt for any wood that was dry and could be used to make a decent fire. We were in some support trenches and I said to other people I was with "I'm going off to find some decent fire-wood." Just a little way back, that is between our support trench and the reserve line, I noticed what had been a farm-building, now a wreckage in the main owing to shell-fire. No individual of any sort was about but I noticed one bit of this wreckage, a byre or out-house of some sort, still stood & its roofing appeared to be intact & its walling undamaged, at least from a little distance. I thought Now that looks to be most likely the very place where there might be not only wooden objects of one sort or another, broken cart-wheels or other discarded bits of timber but, with a bit of luck, a wood-store perfectly dry and cut ready for use. So I went to investigate and when I came close to the wall and found there were signs of its having been a bit more knocked about than appeared from a few hundred yards away, but there *was no door or opening of any sort on that side; but I found a crack against which I put my eye expecting to see either empty darkness or that I should have to go round to the other side of the little building to find an entrance. But what I saw through the small gap in the wall was not the dim emptiness I had expected, but the back of a sacerdos in a gilt-hued planeta, two points of flickering candle-light no doubt lent an extra sense of goldness to the vestment & a golden warmth seemed, by the same agency, to lend the white altar-cloths and the white linen of the celebrant's alb & amice & maniple (the latter, I notice, has been abandoned, without a word of explanation, by these blasted reformers). You can imagine what a great marvel it was for me to see through that chink in the wall. And kneeling in the hay beneath the improvised* mensa *were a few huddled figures in khaki . . . There was a big-bodied Irishman & an Italian naturalised Englishman represented under the forms of Bomber Mulligan and Runner Meotti in* IN PAREN. *on page 121 & Mulligan as "old sweat Mulligan" on page 117 & one or two others. I cant recall at what part of the Mass it was as I looked through that squint-hole and I didn't think I ought to stay long as it seemed rather like an uninitiated bloke prying on the the Mysteries of a Cult. But it made a big impression on me . . . I felt immediately that oneness between the Offerand and those toughs that clustered round him in the dim lit byre—a thing I had never felt remotely as a Protestant at the Office of Holy Communion in spite of the insistence in Protestant theology on "the priesthood of the laity". I then had to seek elsewhere for my fire-wood—I cant remember what I managed to gather.'*

The David of those days would have been ignorant of the word 'anamnesis', of which he was later to make so much use. We have just had it, in an earlier quotation, applied to Mary Magdalen, and what David saw through that chink in the candle-lit building was to become for

him the supreme anamnesis. And this is where
the reader comes in; for the other half of
anamnesis is recognition: that which the reader
gives in return to the poet, and in which he finds
delight, a delight that increases as the reader's
contribution is the fruit of wider reading, greater
sensibility and greater skill in interpretation. The
delight in recognition, and the pathos of recognition, are as old, and older than, Homer and
Vergil. We remember (and reading David reminds
us) how Odysseus, still a stranger at the court of
Alcinous, was moved to tears when the minstrel
sang of the fall of Troy and of how Odysseus
himself raged in the tremendous conflict (this
again we recognise when we look at a little
drawing of David's, a young girl, armoured, on a
white horse, with small ships—a typically Davidian
reference—in the far background, and beneath it
the wording *'Holy Joan of France, defend us in the
tremendous conflict'*)—and there can be few who do
not remember Vergil's overwhelmingly magnifi-
cent 'retractatio' of Homer, when the ship-
wrecked Aeneas gazes on the work of the
'artifices' who have pictured in Dido's new-built
temple the terrible deeds on the windy plain—
the passage which encloses that line so quoted as
to be patient now of no more than a hint—the
lacrimae rerum which no man can translate, and
which Jackson Knight takes six lines to paraphrase.
David is both poet and reader; this Homeric-
Vergilian pathos of recognition runs through his
work. As a reader he has known this joy of
recognition, and as a poet he can hardly write a
line in which we, the readers, do not have to
co-operate with the poet in re-creating through
recognition. This is what we really mean by

tradition: a taking up and a handing on in which both parties share; and when David speaks of the artifex to-day as an Ishmael, it is in this direction, in joining the poet in the wilderness, that hope must lie.

The second half of the initial question about the THE ANATHEMATA—what does it *contain*—cannot be answered as it can when asked of IN PARENTHESIS. The framework of the contents of the latter is determined by the facts of personal experience; for the former the poet had available a vast store of events, images, recollections spread throughout the whole history of western man, and focusing ultimately on three points, the cenacle, Rome, and the island of Britain. There is a succinct if erratic summary of what the poet chose, by Michael Alexander, in the David Jones issue of Agenda, a somewhat longer one, with some difference of emphasis, in the same issue, and a much more detailed exposition in David Blamires's book; and there is no need, I think, to repeat what may be read elsewhere. At least one more piece, however, should be mentioned: an example of Davidian exploration by Jeremy Hooker in THE ANGLO-WELSH REVIEW (vol. 22, no. 50), which shows how to *read* the poem, and how, though hounds may be at fault occasionally they pull down their fox in the end: to which let me attach, in order to show how little a summary can tell of the unendingly expansible content, a fragment of David's own exegesis. It concerns the central section of the book, The Lady of the Pool: and it should be remembered that even this is no more than an interjected comment:

'. . . the Lady of P. is herself an amalgam of many figures—from a waterside tart of sorts to the tutelary figure of London, as, say, Aphrodite of the city of Thebes or Athene of Athens. Certainly she is Britannia at one point. But primarily she is a woman, a lavender-seller talking to an "ancient mariner" from the mediterranean and telling him about London and its tradition and about the voyagers she had met with and the tales they had told her. In the main the setting is toward the end of the middle-ages. There were a number of reasons necessitating this. For one thing she had to represent to some extent the British sea-thing which rose only after the end of the 15th cent. so that the figure had to combine the Hogarthian, Turneresque even Dickensian worlds with the Catholic world of "Dick Whittington", Chaucer, Langland, Geoffrey of Monmouth's Trojan-London myth and so on. Consequently the inter-penetration backwards and forwards and up and down of all the images, historical, legendary and mythological (both the Xtian Mythos and the non-Xtian) must be taken as the main subject of this section. The L. of the P. is telling the tale (in more ways than one!) regarding her own life (i.e. the life of London) and boasting of the various voyages she has heard about to a voyager, to wit this captain, the padrone from the Middle Sea. In the course of which tale-telling on her part all sorts of explicitly Xtian things are of necessity brought in. The captain himself speaks once only on page 141 when in reply to her direct query: "storm or hurricane?" he answers: "For certain this Barke was Tempest tost".

The spelling and the caps here are because that is how W.S. spelt it in (folio) the MACBETH episode of the witches' curse on the sea-captain, the Master of the Tiger who had sailed to Aleppo. Cf. ref. on p. 137 top line to "the Master of the Mary". But this barque made port after enduring all that the elements etc., etc., could work upon it, but limping into port this barque is seen to be hulled "seven times". The water pours however from the starboard side—the "right side" because of a latere dextro. For here both Our Lord and his Mother are, *if only obscurely, implied. That's why on p. 137 it is: "one morning very early on the second day of the week at the rising, the dawn began but whiles it were yet but darkish". Here I used bits of each of the four evangelists' accounts of the hour of the Resurrection, and the ship comes to port on the morning of the Fst. of the Annunciation, so the mass of Gabriel containing the Ave has already been said. The dry wood is becoming lissom and things in general are beginning to look up.'*

Before moving on to David's THE SLEEPING LORD, it may be well to speak of THE BOOK OF BALAAM'S Ass, which is included in that collection but was written between IN PARENTHESIS and THE ANATHE-MATA, or rather was salvaged from a large quantity of material dating from that time. David himself speaks of BALAAM'S Ass as *'affording a link of sorts between two widely separated books'*. I am uncertain whether he is speaking of separation in kind, but I would prefer to regard it as purely chronological, for the peaks of IN PARENTHESIS run on without interruption into the great mountain range of THE ANATHEMATA. BALAAM'S Ass is much nearer in its method of writing to the earlier than to the later poem. Like IN PARENTHESIS, it has a greater simplicity of form (and, indeed, of content: though here again the reader should beware of over-confidence, lest he miss much that calls for objective or subjective gloss); and, again like IN PARENTHESIS, it is attached to the 1914 war. It soon becomes apparent, however, that, as the date is later, so, too, the terrain differs from the battered woods of the Somme in July 1916. That terrible plain of BALAAM'S Ass

'as level as Barking, and as bare as your palm, as trapped and decoyed as a Bannockburn frontage for 300 yards below his

glacis . . . not a bush, no brick-bat, not any accidental and advantageous fold, no lie of dead ground the length of a body . . . not a rock to cleft for, not a spare drift of soil for the living pounds of all their poor bodies drowned in the dun sea',

indicates the ghastly 'Third Ypres', which Liddell Hart calls the *'last scene in the gloomiest drama of British military history',* and to which is attached the dreadful name of Passchendaele: where men did indeed drown in the 'dun sea' of mud.

As the framework of the last part of IN PARENTHESIS is the attack on Mametz Wood, so that of BALAAM'S ASS is an attack, from which but three men returned.

'There was no help for them either on that open plain because the virtue of the land was perished and there was not grass but only broken earth and low foliage of iron; and from the tangled spread of the iron hedge hung the garments peculiar to the men of Ireland and their accoutrements, and the limbs and carcases of the Irish were stretched on some of the iron bushes, because the men of Ireland had made an attempt on the Mill in the early Spring of '15 and again in high summer by express command of the G.O.C. in C. So that the Mill was named on English trench maps: Irish Mill, but on enemy maps it was called Aachen Haus. And as there was no help for the men of Ireland so there was no help for the men of Britain [i.e. for the London Welsh R.W.F., once again committed] *. . . and with field-glasses it was possible to discern . . . the chequered cloth of the men of Lower Britain.'*

Here again we meet David's catholicity of compassion. Irish, English, Welsh, Scottish, German— with a continual backward look to Roman and Romano-British—are all covered with a mantle of tenderness, even though there is no Queen of the Woods to '*cut bright boughs of various flowering*' for the dead[1]—no Emil to be given a curious crown of golden saxifrage, no dead Hansel to share dog-violets with Goronwy: for 'his' structure

'*is of re-inforced concrete, the loopholes are of the best pattern and well disposed so as to afford the maximum sweep of fire, the approaches are secured by a triple belt and his trip-wire is cunningly staked*'.

Those few words, '*the men of Ireland . . . the men of Britain . . . the men of Lower Britain*' brought together in that one place, recall the whole range of Irish-Welsh-Anglo-French epic literature, and the inclusion of 'pounds' in 'the living pounds' adds, by its slang, a wry but kindly humour that belongs peculiarly to that one war period, and to that one type of infantryman.

BALAAM'S ASS is so much shorter than IN PARENTHESIS and has been in circulation for so much shorter a time, that it is reasonable to write of it in rather more detail; but what is said of its quality applies equally well to the earlier book, and indeed to the whole of his work—for all his life he has been writing the same book and painting the same picture. And yet, as in all true unity, each component retains its own differentiating essence.

---

[1] Reverting to IN PARENTHESIS, Robert Graves's account of his going into Mametz Wood a few days after the attack and climbing over 'the wreckage of green branches' is a confirmation of the aptness of David's imagery.

This component is no mere description of horror, for running through the texture are two strands, one of humour and one which I can describe only as a grandeur of cosmic concept: an awareness of the inter-connection of all things, great and small, of an all-embracing unity in which all is cared for, of what in a different context one would call a pleroma. It is what we had in mind when we said in the Christmas Preface: *nova mentis nostrae oculis lux tuae claritatis infulsit, ut dum visibiliter Deum cognoscimus, per hunc in invisibilium amorem rapiamur*—the particular concrete things of here and now expanding into the one and perennial. And the second strand: when I say 'humour' it is because I am at a loss for a word which will cover not only wit but an amused delight—almost that quality we read into 'Cum eo eram cuncta componens . . .' boldly but aptly translated by Knox as, *'I was at his side, a master-workman, my delight increasing with each day, as I made play with him all the while: made play in this world of dust, with the sons of Adam for my play-fellows.'*

It is the transition from one strand to the other, often sudden, never shocking (though I must confess that the horror of the reference to Hector, with its really terrible double meaning and double level of speech, slang and epic

'you Hector, whose arse they couldn't see for dust at the circuit of the wall'

is almost too much for me)—it is this transition which is eminently skilful and beautiful. Thus, BALAAM's Ass builds up to a far-reaching litany of all those upon whom the dying called. Weaving in and out of the solemnity (with the full, Vergilian, sense of *sollemnis*) is the at once pathetic and laughter-provoking account of the escapes of the three survivors, Pussy (earlier, Squib) Lucifer, Pick-em-up-Shenkin and Dodger (earlier Ducky) Austin: and the cry is not only to *'that creature of water . . . to gentle Margaret . . . to Joan the Maid that keeled the pot . . . Brigit the Kildare maid . . .'* but also to *'God the Father of Heaven . . . who knows best how to gather his epiklesis from that open plain, who transmutes their cheerless blasphemy into a lover's word, who spoke by Balaam and by Balaam's Ass, who spoke also by Sgt. Bullock . . .* (I was about to stop there, but glancing back at the book I was overcome by the reference to the wounded Aphrodite, and must include . . .) *. . . on her that wept for a wounded palm that she got by a mortal spear'*. This litany is between three and four pages in length, and in that space it packs, cunningly fitted, interlaced, harmoniously fash- ioned, mutations and permutations of reference that build up into a vast and tremendously moving monument to all that is sacred.

V

The Sleeping Lord

THE SLEEPING LORD was published in March 1974.
It brings together all that had then been printed,
sporadically, of David's work since THE ANATHE-
MATA, twenty-two years earlier, except 'The
Narrows' (in the ANGLO-WELSH REVIEW, autumn
1973) and a draft of 'The Kensington Mass' (the
second AGENDA D. J. issue, 1974). David calls these
nine pieces fragments, but the word can hardly
be used here in the sense in which it is applied,
for example, to the fragments of Ennius (I choose
Ennius, not a very good example, because that
dogged old hexametrist is specially dear to
David). THE BOOK OF BALAAM'S ASS, it is true,
starts with a ragged edge, but the context is
restored and the continuity established in a very
few lines. And the other eight sections form a
complete whole, each separate 'fragment' a
'squared, dressed stone' in the orderly structure.

The collection falls into four parts: an intro-
ductory poem, 'A, a, a, Domine Deus', which
comes close to, but leaves a loophole from
despair; then four sections, 'The Wall', 'The
Dream of Private Clitus', 'The Fatigue', and 'The
Tribune's Visitation', which have in common an
imperial Roman setting; then comes 'The Tutelar
of the Place', which may be read as a prayer
against the imposition of uniformity at the
expense of diversity and personality; and this
acts as a bridge to the two 'Welsh' sections, 'The
Hunt' and 'The Sleeping Lord'.

The opening poem gives us the theme of the book: a lament for all that is lost by *Gleichschaltung* —a word which David uses later, its literal meaning (I take it) having an elasticity which covers all that distinguishes the 'fact-man' from the 'signifer', the technocrat from the artefactor, with, maybe, a further bestiality born of its Nazi association. It covers, too, our old dialectical friend, who destroys the very thing which he seeks to build, by his very success in building it; by imposing conformity instead of true unity, he kills diversity and produces our modern fragmentation; by developing man's technological powers, he kills the artefact. It is interesting that Maritain uses the opening cry (A, a, a, Domine Deus) in a different, but allied context. He has been saying that art expresses what our ideas cannot express; '*A, a, a,*' cries Jeremiah, '*Domine Deus, ecce nescio loqui, quia puer ego sum*' (*I do not know how to speak, for I am but a boy*). David restores the cry to a modern situation which is parallel to that in which the twenty-year old prophet found himself when he was called upon to denounce a different cor- ruption of spirituality 2,600 years ago. This intensely moving poem is saved from utter despair only by being a prayer: for where there is prayer there must be hope. Will we see '*the Living God projected from the Machine*'? Will '*the perfected steel be my sister*'? This was a problem discussed by David and his friends ever since the twenties and thirties, without any answer being found that was not catastrophe: yet the mere fact that the problem itself can be the material for an artefact must indicate that somehow, some time, man will re-emerge. There is a curious little passage in 'The Narrows':

'I wonder how the Dialectic
*   works far-side the Styx*
or if blithe Helen toes the Party Line
*   and white Iope and the Dog*
if the withering away
is more remarked
*   than hereabouts.'*

I do not think it is being over-fanciful to re-transfer the dialectic to this side the Styx, and to take comfort in the assurance that the *trivial intersections,* the *dead forms causation projects from pillar to pylon,* the *automatic devices,* the *inane patterns,* must contain their own contradiction, with a new synthesis, still human, to emerge at a higher level. David does no more than hint at this (in the Preface to IN PARENTHESIS, p. xiv):

'It would be interesting to know how we shall ennoble our new media as we have already ennobled and made significant our old—candle-light, fire-light, Cups, Wands and Swords, to choose at random.'

The next four sections. 'The Wall', 'The Dream of Private Clitus', 'The Fatigue' and 'The Tribune's Visitation', may be taken together. They are each a close-up of the hateful process at work, though the 'Dream' pictures the reality of which the process is a contradiction. In 'The Wall', a Roman legionary, puzzled, devoted, humorous, resigned, sarcastic, laments the degradation of the Roman ideal—as Jeremiah, of the opening poem, cried out against the coarsening of Jewish spirituality. Consider, with the lines that follow, a representation of a Roman military *signum:*

*Erect, crested with the open fist that turns the evil spell, lifting
the flat palm that disciplines the world, the signa lift in
disciplined acknowledgement, the eagles stand erect for Ilia.*
                    O Roma
                    O Ilia
                    Io Triumphe, Io, Io . . .
                    the shopkeepers presume to make
the lupine cry their own.
                        The magnates of the Boarium
*leave their nice manipulations. You may call the day ferial,
rub shoulders with the plebs. All should turn out to see how
those appointed to die take their Roman medicine . . .*

—and follow up, I beg you, the implications of

'the maimed king in his tinctured vesture, the dying tegernos
of the wasted landa *well webbed in our marbled parlour,
bitched and bewildered and far from his dappled* patria *far
side the misted Fretum'.*

The *retiarius,* with his net, the spider, 'tinctis
vestibus de Bosra', the Waste Land of the maimed
king in Malory and the Mabinogion, infantry
slang of the war, the 'Dying Gaul'—these (and the
list is not exhaustive) are brought together and
made into one with a true 'carpentry of song'.

With a characteristic change of level, the poet
slides into nobler heights when he asks (the
enthusiasm of the learned craftsman passing, as
often in David's writing, into the unlettered
ranker):

            did the bright share
                            turn the dun clod
        to the star plan

> did they parcel out
>
> *per scamna et strigas*
>
> the civitas *of God*
>
> *that we should sprawl*
>
> *from Septimontium*
>
> *a megalopolis that wills death?*

—and finally, with a dreadful sigh, he returns to duty. At first reading the language may appear completely straightforward, but a closer examination discloses so intricate a pattern that every line lends itself—like the 'Mantuan's ordered mine of meaning'—to an endlessly fruitful exegesis. As another random example may serve the single phrase 'the troia'd wandering'—consider the depth of the adjective: the Homeric association (both Iliad and Odyssey), Aeneas and Vergil, the boys' formalised ride in the fifth Aeneid (and what of the Royal Horse Artillery's tremendous ballet?), the labyrinth, the Sibyl and all the related hares Jackson Knight puts up in CUMAEAN GATES.

Almost as a by-product there comes into 'The Wall' the character of this fellow with the rooty-medal up. There is a similar unstressed, 'thrown-away', characterisation in IN PARENTHESIS. Plato says that the divine mania without which the man who has *techné* alone will knock in vain at the gates of poetry, visits only the soul which is *hapalé* and *abatos* (we might say, in words that are— no, that used to be, familiar, to many of us, *mitis* and *intemerata*): and may we not apply those words to the young soldier, John Ball, and recognise in him the gentle, wide-eyed, innocent, so much younger than his calendar years, painter represented in the quasi-self-portrait of 1931, entitled (matter again for thought) 'Human Being' which is reproduced on the cover of WORD AND IMAGE IV?[1] Such characterisation is even more notice-able in the kindly Private Clitus, who describes his dream to a young Greek recruit as they serve their spell of duty on the wall of Jerusalem: and over the whole looms the emperor's *Vare, Vare, redde legiones*; for the dream came to Clitus as he slept, bivouacked in the Teutoburg Forest, where *'these big, fair-hued square-heads had hung on our exposed flank for five days'*. The dream presents a different, if dream-land, vision of Rome, Terra Mater, of great sweetness—echoing the sweetness that is found in the Lady of the Pool section of IN PARENTHESIS: and (an elegant, if endlessly debat-able touch) it is from the gate of *horn* that the dream emerges. It ends in a fine fusion of humour and mystery with the introduction of the hateful, sly, time-serving, calculating, aptly named C.S.M. (if that is something like the equivalent rank) Brasso, whose mother

> *'was ventricled of bronze*
> *had ubera of iron*
> *and [they say] that at each vigilia's term*
> *she gave him of her lupine nectar*
> *and by numbers.'*

And yet
> *'That'ld be a difficult thing to dream, Oenomaus:*
> *Dea Roma, Flora Dea*
>
> *meretrix or world-nutricula*
> *without Brasso.*

---

[1] Published by the National Book League, and referred to earlier.

> There are some things
>
> *that can't be managed*
>
> *even in these dreams.'*

So the book (for, to my mind, it can be taken as a single unit) builds up to its first climax in 'The Fatigue', where the scene is again Jerusalem, the time just before the Passion of Christ. It is a wonderfully bold concept to treat that cosmic act from the point of view of the common soldiers detailed for what is to them but one more fatigue. It is introduced by a short poem, 'Gwanwyn yn y llwyn' *(Primavera in the woodland?)* which brings sudden radiance into this sombre landscape. It is, moreover, a fine example of David's power of assimilation and re-presentation, and at the same time of opening doors that lead to ever more distant *agalmata*—and I use that word to describe objects of delight—as Penelope's keepsake to Odysseus was to 'be for him an *agalma*'—because of the glittering quality (with the glitter of Odysseus' engraved golden brooch) of this short poem, and because of the connection between the two words *agalmata* and *anathemata;* for to Homer the contributions of the poet to the ceremonial meal were *anathemata* or *agalmata daitos;* and it as well to remember (a point to which David himself refers somewhere) that the *anathemata* are not only the things held up 'for a remembering' but also the things *made* to give delight.

'*Arbor axed . . .*' the poem starts, and the first line takes us straight to the 'Dream of the Rood' and the 'Vexilla Regis', to 'Crux fidelis' *('fronde, flore, germine')* and Ennius, so to Homer and Vergil, and

73

again to David's own work (cf. the reference noted above, to 'a latere dextro', in connection with the Lady of the Pool, and the 'Dream of the Rood's' *'swaetan on tha swithran healfe'*; cf., too the *'dreaming arbor / ornated regis purpura'* of *Sherthursdaye and Venus Day*—and the inscription opposite that passage—p. 240).

'Vexilla' sends us to *'Pange lingua gloriosi Proelium certaminis'*, which in turn sends us to Aquinas's borrowing in *'pange lingua gloriosi Corporis mysterium'*; and the densely-packed doctrinal content of Aquinas's hymn reminds us of the element of teaching or education in all poetry of the first order. It reminds us, too, again in David's work and in his presentation of his central theme, of the particular weight of the word 'recumbent' as it occurs in the closing lines of THE ANATHEMATA ('recumbens cum fratribus'—and the 'turba' is there, too, and what David calls Nelson's *ecclesia*); so that we have a direct succession, Homer, Ennius, Vergil, Fortunatus with the 'Dream of the Rood', Aquinas, David. And yet these few lines are but a splinter in the great beam that supports David's work.

'The Fatigue' is a daring piece. The men are told off for their duty by an N.C.O. who rattles out the almost liturgically compulsory sarcasms and witticisms of the parade-ground. The solemnity of the occasion is introduced unobtrusively by a reference to the Water Gate *('. . . when you have entered the city a man carrying a jar of water will meet you' . . .')*. One of the men reports, from outside his sector, *'a movement out beyond the Water Gate'*, and brings down upon himself.

'*And you can report for optio's party, immediate, on relief of guard, that's now. He wants a few extra details at the Water Gate and seeing you're so attracted to the Water Gate, why then, for once in y'r twenty years service your duties may fit your desires.*'

Gradually the sergeant's language shifts into a higher gear (I would have avoided that metaphor, had I not noticed that David uses it himself) until the awful majesty of the occasion becomes apparent: and the poet takes advantage of the Celtic origin of one of the soldiers detailed to express the climactic words (*'the place of the skull'*) in Welsh:

> *in that place*
> *which little Ginger the Mountain*
> > *the Pretanic fatigue-wallah*
> > *(shipped in a slaver to Corbilo-on-Liger)*
> *calls in his lingo*
> > *Lle'r Benglog.*

This comes as a vast explosion, as though the heavens had indeed been rent asunder. And then a sudden deflation: back to the vast, sprawling, impersonal administrative machine which initiates in the heart of megalopolis the process which comes down, step by step, and decides that for *this* man and *that* man

> *By your place on a sergeant's roster*
> *by where you stand in y'r section*
> *by when you fall in*
> *by if they check you from left or right*
> *by a chance numbering-off*
> > *by a corporal's whim*

you will furnish
that Fatigue.

At the Mermaid Theatre in London, in April 1974, Douglas Cleverdon produced a reading of David's poetry which included 'The Fatigue', read by an Englishman, Frank Duncan, a Welshman, Aubrey Richards, and an Anglo-Welshman, David himself (the last from a recording). Frank Duncan reproduced perfectly the steely, slightly sadistic, sarcastic tone of the N.C.O. When the Welshman moved into the climax, he was as though possessed by the piece, building up the tension to the thunderbolt of *Lle'r Benglog*. And this was followed by David's deep, measured, deliberate, carefully enunciated utterance, with a metallic edge, carrying the poem remorselessly to its conclusion in *you will furnish that Fatigue*.

After a long spell of hard and dangerous service, the old soldier not only develops a contempt for bull, but may even begin to question the very foundation for which he serves. Hence, in part at least, the Tribune's (Brigadier's?) visitation. He has come, unexpected, to stamp out—not by severity *(I've never been one for the vine-stick, I've never been a sergeant-major "Hand-me-another" to any man')* but by reasoned explanation, a hankering for what is particular, diverse and local: *'the remembered things of origin and streamhead, the things of the beginnings, of our own small beginnings'*. It is the 'fact-man's' apology. *'We serve contemporary fact'*, he reminds his men, and it is their duty to

'discipline the world-floor / to a common level / till every presuming difference / and all the sweet remembered demarca-

tions / wither / to the touch of us / and know the fact of empire'. There is great pathos in this address, for the tribune himself is only too dearly aware of how precious are the 'bumpkin sacraments'. *'No dying Gaul / figures in the rucked circus sand / his far green valley / more clear than do I figure / from this guard-house door / a little porch below Albanus.'*

Here we see portrayed, both in its majesty and its horror, the same monster against the later form of which the poet cries out in *A, a, a, Domine Deus*: the barren uniformity which can ruthlessly insist that 'only the neurotic look to their beginnings'. And again, with admirable audacity, David ends, through the medium of the tribune's final words, with a devastating parody of the Pauline doctrine of the mystical body. Almost every word in the last page of the 'Visitation' is a heart-chilling reflection, as though in a distorting mirror, of everything that is most sacred to man: all the more terrible in that the speaker is a reasonable and kindly man.

Here again, with the transition to 'The Tutelar of the Place', we have to recognise the structural unity of this collection; for we pass on to an invocation of her who

'loves place, time, demarcation, hearth, kin, enclosure, site, differentiated cult, though she is but one mother of us all'.

Again it is a prayer that is saved from despair by the fact that the prayer can still be made, that there is still some gleam of hope:

'In all times of Gleichschaltung, *in the days of the central*

economies, set up the hedges of illusion round some remnant of us.'

The tenderness of the writing, the sense of possible comfort, the love and respect for what is individually real, rooted, warm, for the stuff of which those are made of whom it is said that they shall inherit the earth—this, particularly because it comes hard upon the fact-man's cold and inflexible iconoclasm—this is intensely moving and, to my mind, supremely beautiful.

It takes the reader back to the treatment of the beginnings of things in the first part of the ANATHEMATA, 'Rite and Foretime', and in particular to the continuation of the passage quoted earlier which prompted a reference to Vergilian imagery. We may set side by side as examples of true pathos the introduction of

'Little Hissarlik / least of acclivities / yet / high as Hector the Wall / high as Helen the Moon / who, being lifted up / draw the West to them'

(echoed in the 'Tutelar') and another passage from Vergil. Here Vergil introduces us to something very small, very dear, and the beginning of something which was to be very great. In the eighth Aeneid (364 f.) Evander, standing with Aeneas on the site of what, unknown to them, was to be Rome, welcomes his guest in lines that moved Dryden to the grand comment, *'For my part, I am lost in the admiration of it: I contemn the world when I think of it, and myself when I translate it.'* '. . . *rebusque veni non asper egenis'.*—David's pathos can stand with that, and he may well share with Vergil Dryden's beautifully worded praise.

So far, then, in the SLEEPING LORD, we have had the problem stated, the case argued, the prayer spoken. Now we pass into the poetry of application as, with 'The Hunt' and 'The Sleeping Lord' we enter *'these whoreson Marchlands of this Welshry'*. When St. Guthlac felt his way up-river to Crowland (cf. ANATHEMATA, p. 112), *'hearing the speech of the surviving Britons, he thought it the language of devils'*. Readers who have English alone and are unwilling to make the effort required by the shift from the pronunciation of English to that of Welsh—even with the annotated help provided—should encourage themselves to do so by reading or re-reading the essay on 'The Myth of Arthur' in EPOCH AND ARTIST, and the Rees CELTIC HERITAGE. To minds that are governed by a purely English tradition—which skips over what is originally British in our culture—even the Mabinogion is a strange book (as, even more, is the related Irish epic) in comparison with Malory. And such a reader naturally gravitates to and finds himself more at home in 'Peredur' than he does in the 'Four Branches'—for which he has to accept the superciliousness of the Welsh scholars. In such cases, as David argues most convincingly, the fault is ours. We are blind both to that particular period, unique in Western European history, when the Arthurian myth was born from the last struggle of the Romano-Britons in their abandoned island, and to the dim recessions into which the Celtic imagination disappears. This is what David has in mind when he blames Tennyson not for what he put into the Arthurian legend (for he rightly 'invested the subject with the values of his own age') but for what he left out. Sliding, as he often does when the pressure builds up, into poetry, David puts the matter in a form that is more cogent than argument:

'From Chrétien to Malory we are aware of unplumbed deeps and recessions below and beyond the medievalised and christianised story. Gusts drive down upon us through sudden rifts in the feudal vaulting, up through the Angevin floor; we stumble among twisted roots of primeval growth among traceries of Gothic and Christian workmanship. Behind the contemporary "sets", the ever recurring "passing meek gentle-woman" complete in the paraphernalia of medieval high life . . . we scent things of another order . . . Could we remove the Gothic attire, the figure beneath would be very other than that of "a fair lady and thereto lusty and young". Rather we should see displayed the ageless, powerful, vaticinal, mistress of magic, daubed with ochre, in the shift of divination, at the gate of the labyrinth.'

There, indeed, the leaves flutter, and we may say that 'clear the cipher runs from Cumae, though hinge creak and wind scatter manic fronds'. It is this reaching back into the dimmest caves of the folk-mind that fascinates the archaeologists who delight in David's work. And that is why Ireland, as in the Mabinogion, feels so close—and, incidentally, it adds something peculiarly moving to the battle-scenes of IN PARENTHESIS and BALAAM'S ASS, when we remember the Irish heroism on that first day of July and in the earlier attack on the Mill, with, on each occasion, what the Mabinogion calls the Men of the Island of the Mighty and the men in the chequered cloth of Lower Britain.

It is the same, of course, with Old English. We may be obliged at first to read 'The Dream of the Rood' in translation, but even a slightly better knowledge of the language brings an enrichment that runs through the whole of our reading—and can affect even our visual perception in, for example, David's use of

'Ongyrede Hine tha geong haeled thaet waes God aelmihtig'

. . . both in an inscription and as an immensely fruitful source in, among other places, the final section of THE ANATHEMATA: as an illumination, too, of Fortunatus' 'Arbor decora et fulgida' and so of David's 'Primavera in the Woodland' and so of all the Passion-centred poetry of THE SLEEPING LORD.

It is the Culhwch and Olwen story from the Mabinogion which provides the matter for 'The Hunt', and it has to be read if one is to appreciate how David has imposed his own loves, sources of amusement and peculiar pathos on the ancient framework. A characteristic detail is an example, taken almost at random, of the grand and time-worn with conversational and workaday. The poet is listing those who rode out to hunt the great Boar:

'if there were riders from the Faithful Fetter-locked War-Band
there were riders also from the Three Faithless War-Bands;
the riders who receive the shaft-shock
in place of their radiant lords
the riders who slip the column
whose lords alone
receive the shafts.'

The three words 'slip the column' give a change of emphasis, context and association which strengthens the link between the Welsh prince's retinue and the fusilier. For 'The Hunt' we have the advantage of David's own reading on a gramophone record, which contains extracts also from IN PARENTHESIS and THE ANATHEMATA; and with it a valuable note from David about all three. Of *The Hunt* he says, after speaking of the Culhwch and Olwen story and the war-bands of the Island led by an Arthur-figure:

'. . . *what distinguishes this native prose tale from the subsequent great medieval Arthurian Romance-Cycles is its vivid sense of the particular, of locality and site . . .'*

The same may be applied to 'The Sleeping Lord' itself. To us, at home in the romanticised anglo-continental tradition of chivalry, the Arthur, *rex quondam rexque futurus,* is a very different figure from the sleeping lord, and the fund of knowledge the reader must acquire covers wide tracts of pre-history, geology and the origins of myth and folk-lore. Nor can maps be neglected, for the vast figure is seen as literally covering and guarding the whole of that special third of Britain. At the same time, David lets loose his peculiar facility for the particular image, the sharply drawn, the visually individualised. The descriptions of the king's retainers, the Foot-holder, the Candle-bearer, the Priest, each introduces a special person, performing a special sacred function, with the delicacy in the construction of detail that you find in his drawing, super-imposed upon or blended with his use of colour. And yet, no accumulations of intricacies ever check the fluidity with which the whole comes together; you can never use of the work the word which David often uses of an unsuccessful picture, his own or another's, when he says that *'it wont do—it's tight.'*

David is fond of a pattern which builds up to a first climax, like Dai's boast in In Parenthesis, like The Lady of the Pool in The Anathemata, and like the shattering *Lle'r Benglog* of the 'Fatigue':

> *There, in that place*
> > *that will be called*
> > *the Tumulus*
> *you will complete the routine*

—a first climax which is followed by a more meditative passage, which again boils up to the final climax. Here, in the 'Sleeping Lord', we find a well-contrived change. The climax comes when the Priest, praying for all the *'departed of the universal orbis'*, murmurs *'requiem aeternam dona eis, domine'*: and the Candle-bearer, unable to contain himself,

'sings out in a high, clear and distinct voice the respond ET LUX PERPETUA LUCEAT EIS'.

The sleep of the lord, and of the land that sleeps, is assumed into the eternal rest of Paradise—with just a hint (and here again we meet David's use of the immediate and contemporary in the heart of the perennial—when the sentinels wonder *'what's on the west wind'*, and *'whether these broken dregs of Troea yet muster'*—the sentinels on the Hay Bluff we know)— with just a hint of the rex futurus. And the poem ends with that hush, dear to Vergil as the ending of a book. The hush contained in the last line of the Second Aeneid—*Cessi et sublato montis genitore petivi*—the quiet finality of the first word, and the suggestion of expectation that follows, these I find again in the ending of 'The Sleeping Lord':

> Does the land wait the sleeping lord
> or is the wasted land
> that very lord who sleeps?

Postscript

David Jones was included in the 1974 Birthday Honours as a Companion of Honour, to the delight of his friends. Readers of his essay 'Wales and the Crown' will understand his own delight in being the object of the Queen's personal choice.

The above was written while David Jones still lived, in the care of the Blue Nuns, at Harrow-on-the-Hill in Middlesex. There he died, on 28th October 1974. I have left my words as they were written, to be, as it were, in the present tense. His work is instinct with love of, and with the remembrance of, all men, all women, all children, all creation. What he often expressed as a wish for others, never more magnificently than in the peculiarly Welsh setting of 'The Sleeping Lord', *Lux perpetua luceat eis,* is now for him eternal fact.

A Selected Bibliography

DAVID JONES.

IN PARENTHESIS, 1937.

THE ANATHEMATA, 1952

EPOCH AND ARTIST (selected writings, edited by Harman Grisewood), 1959.

(These three are also published as paper-backs, all by Faber & Faber.)

AN INTRODUCTION TO THE RIME OF THE ANCIENT MARINER, London, Clover Hill Editions, 1972.

THE SLEEPING LORD AND OTHER FRAGMENTS, 1974, Faber & Faber.

A poem entitled 'The Narrows' is printed in THE ANGLO-WELSH REVIEW, Autumn 1973; and a draft of another, 'The Kensington Mass', in the 1974 David Jones issue of AGENDA.

About David Jones and his work.
David Blamires, DAVID JONES, ARTIST AND WRITER, Manchester University Press, 1971. This treats of both his pictorial and literary work; and contains a 'select bibliography' which includes much more than the adjective might seem to imply.

John H. Johnston, ENGLISH POETRY OF THE FIRST WORLD WAR, Princeton, 1964. The last and longest chapter of this is 'The Heroic Vision: David Jones'.

Roland Bouyssou, LES POÈTES-COMBATTANTS ANGLAIS DE LA GRANDE GUERRE. University of Toulouse, 1974. Chapter VII is 'La Geste de David Jones'.

Robert Speaight, THE LIFE OF ERIC GILL, London, Methuen, 1966.

Donald Attwater, A CELL OF GOOD LIVING, the Life, Works and Opinions of Eric Gill, London, Geoffrey Chapman, 1969.
(The two above are concerned with David Jones indirectly but none the less fruitfully.)

PERIODICALS

David Blamires's bibliography covers these, but there have been a couple of important additions since his book was published: two special David Jones issues, one of AGENDA (1974), and the other of POETRY WALES (1972); and the Autumn 1973 issue of THE ANGLO-WELSH REVIEW.

BROADCASTS AND RECORDINGS

There is an article by Douglas Cleverdon in the POETRY WALES issue about the presentation of David's work through the medium of the human voice. David's own voice can be heard on an *Argo* record (PLP 1093), which contains extracts from

THE ANATHEMATA and IN PARENTHESIS, and the whole of 'The Hunt'.

His poems are also read on the Argo record *Poets of Wales—David Jones,* and this includes the poems A, a, a, Domine Deus, The Wall, from 'The Sleeping Lord' and The Tribune's Visitation.

Acknowledgements

First, to David Jones himself, for permission to quote from his letters and (with acknowledgment to Messrs. Faber & Faber also) from his published writings; to Walter Shewring, for what I have borrowed, or rather filched, from him; to Harman Grisewood and his publishers (Messrs. Hutchinson & Co. Ltd.) for permission to quote from ONE THING AT A TIME; to the editor of NEW BLACKFRIARS, for allowing me to reproduce here the substance of a paper on THE SLEEPING LORD which I wrote for him; to Douglas Cleverdon (constant channel for the waters of Helicon); to Mrs. Eleanor Jebb, A. D. Peters & Co. and Messrs. Methuen & Co. for permission to quote from Hilaire Belloc; and to the Welsh Arts Council, to whom I owe the privilege of being allowed to try, to the best of my ability, to write of him who is 'of poets Apersie'.

The Author

René Hague was born in London in 1905, of Irish parents. He was educated and worked in England, mostly as a printer—at first in collaboration with Eric Gill, whose youngest daughter he married. His friendship with David Jones dates back to 1924; it was this close link and his association with Gill that brought him the privilege of printing David's first book, IN PARENTHESIS. Much of his work, too, has been in translations or adaptations (for the old Third Programme of the B.B.C.) from Old French, including a version of THE SONG OF ROLAND which, to his delight, commended itself to David. In later years he has translated many of the writings of Père Teilhard de Chardin. He served with the R.A.F. in the second world war; and returned to Ireland in 1963. He is at present writing an explanatory commentary on THE ANATHEMATA.

This Edition,
designed by Jeff Clements,
is set in Monotype Spectrum 12 Didot on 13 point
and printed on Basingwerk Parchment by
Qualitex Printing Limited, Cardiff

It is limited to 1,000 copies of which this is

Copy No. 771